SIMPLE WA...

Spiritual Life in the Catholic Tradition

Emilie Griffin

A Sheed & Ward Book

ROWMAN & LITTLEFIELD PUBLISHERS, INC.

Lanham • Boulder • New York • Toronto • Oxford

A SHEED & WARD BOOK

ROWMAN & LITTLEFIELD PUBLISHERS, INC.

Published in the United States of America
by Rowman & Littlefield Publishers, Inc.
A wholly owned subsidiary of The Rowman & Littlefield Publishing Group, Inc.
4501 Forbes Boulevard, Suite 200, Lanham, Maryland 20706
www.rowmanlittlefield.com

PO Box 317
Oxford
OX2 9RU, UK

Copyright © 2006 by Emilie Griffin

British Library Cataloguing in Publication Information Available

Library of Congress Cataloging-in-Publication Data

Griffin, Emilie.
    Simple ways to pray : spiritual life in the Catholic tradition / by Emilie
Griffin.
        p. cm.— (The come & see series)
    "A Sheed & Ward book."
    Includes bibliographical references and index.
    ISBN 0-7425-5083-4 (hardcover : alk. paper)—ISBN 0-7425-5084-2
(pbk. : alk. paper)
    1. Spiritual life—Catholic Church. 2. Prayer—Catholic Church. I. Title. II.
Come & see.

BX2178.G75 2005
248.3'2—dc22   2005018900

Printed in the United States of America

♾^TM The paper used in this publication meets the minimum requirements of
American National Standard for Information Sciences—Permanence of Paper
for Printed Library Materials, ANSI/NISO Z39.48-1992.

SIMPLE WAYS TO PRAY

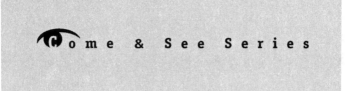

Come & See Series

The **Come & See Series** from Sheed & Ward is modeled on Jesus' compassionate question: "What do you seek?" and his profound invitation to "Come and see" the world through the eyes of faith (John 1:38–39). The series offers spiritual seekers lively, thought-provoking, and accessible books that explore topics of faith and the Catholic Christian tradition. Each book in the series is written by trustworthy guides who are the very best teachers, theologians, and scholars.

Series Editors: James Martin, S.J., and Jeremy Langford

People of the Covenant: An Invitation to the Old Testament
By Dianne Bergant

Who Is Jesus? Why Is He Important?: An Invitation to the New Testament
By Daniel J. Harrington, S.J.

Living Justice: Catholic Social Teaching in Action
By Thomas Massaro, S.J.

Professions of Faith: Living and Working as a Catholic
Edited by James Martin, S.J., and Jeremy Langford

A Faith You Can Live With: Understanding the Basics
By John O'Donnell, S.J.

Bread of Life, Cup of Salvation: Understanding the Mass
By John Baldovin, S.J.

How Do Catholics Read the Bible?
By Daniel J. Harrington, S.J.

Simple Ways to Pray: Spiritual Life in the Catholic Tradition
By Emilie Griffin

To my granddaughter,

Avery Helen Sikes,

who I hope will some day read this book

Contents

Acknowledgments

I n this book I have included some poems of my own as well as translations of Latin hymns and prayers. Brief biblical quotations are from the New American Bible or the New Revised Standard Version. An occasional Bible verse is taken from the King James Version. In using the masculine pronoun for God, I am following traditional biblical usage.

I want to thank my husband William Griffin, a writer and scholar, for his constant support and assistance to me in the completion of this book. My editors, Father James Martin, S.J., and Jeremy Langford, have encouraged me and made fine suggestions. I am grateful to Rev. Msgr. Michael J. Dempsey, long a friend in the spiritual life, for his thoughtful reading of an early draft of this work. My children, Lucy Griffin Sikes, Henry Griffin, and Sarah Griffin Thibodeaux, and my sons-in-law, David Sikes and Troy Thibodeaux, have given me unflagging encouragement.

Opening the Treasure Box

A NEW START

Maybe someone is standing, as I once did, at the threshold of prayer, wondering what prayer is all about.

This person wants to pray, longs for the experience of prayer, but may not know how to begin. Or maybe this person has started already, without much sense of momentum, wondering whether prayer is a gift within reach.

Possibly he or she is busy, over-busy, with far too many commitments and obligations.

For this person I want to open up the treasure box of Catholic tradition, to describe a few of the riches offered by a long history of Christian prayer.

I want to outline the simple steps required to sketch out a spiritual life.

I want to show prayer as a new focusing of our yearnings and energies. I want to accentuate the possibilities prayer will open up: an exciting surprise for beginners and a source of refreshment to those who are already engaged in prayer.

There are dozens of books on prayer, but perhaps not all are fully accessible. The beginner in prayer needs a few points about methods and techniques of prayer. But also she or he needs encouragement to take the plunge, to get involved in the refreshing waters of spiritual life. In this book a vision will be given of what such a life can mean. Those who have already taken the plunge may need to swim farther from shore.

WHY SHOULD I PRAY?

Some questions come to mind right away. Why should I pray? What difference will it make in my life? Is prayer about asking for things? How much time should I spend? How will I find the time? Where should I pray? What if I feel awkward or strange? Is prayer a "family thing"?

What if I'm the only one in my circle interested in prayer?

These and other questions will be considered. At the same time, we will look at the many and varied styles of prayer in the Catholic tradition, styles which are being richly revived today.

WHAT IS PRAYER?

Prayer begins as a deep urgency or longing for something beyond—something greater than ourselves—for God, even though we may not yet be able to name that longing and call it prayer. Many attempts have been made to describe prayer. Spiritual writers and teachers attempt to define—sometimes by a figure of speech or metaphor—what prayer is. Prayer has been called "a raising of the heart and mind to God" and "a long, loving look at the real."

Poets have sometimes attempted to describe prayer. The American poet Emily Dickinson wrote:

> Prayer is the little implement
> Through which men reach
> Where presence is denied them.
>
> They fling their speech
> By means of it in God's ear;
>
> If then he hear
> This sums the apparatus
> Comprised in prayer.[1]

As usual, she is rather witty and concise.

George Herbert, an English country parson, wrote some profound spiritual poems. One gives a long list of comparisons meant to define prayer. Herbert says, for instance, that prayer is "God's breath in man returning to his birth." He means, I think, that prayer originates with God, who breathes into us a spirit of prayer; then we breathe it back toward God. In short, our prayer begins and ends in God. God calls us to pray, and we respond. Prayer is our response to God's initiative.

Herbert also says prayer is "the heart in pilgrimage." Prayer is a yearning of the heart, not a certain reciting of set prayer-formulas. It is genuine, sincere, heartfelt. Another phrase Herbert uses to define prayer is "the soul in paraphrase." What on earth does he mean? Herbert suggests that prayer transforms the soul; no longer your everyday, garden-variety soul, it has been transformed by grace.[2]

Herbert's prayer-poems draw on deep experience. In one of them, called "Mattens" (it is the old spelling for Matins and the old name for Morning Prayer), Herbert reflects on why God should be so concerned with us, why the Almighty would seek us out and give us a desire to pray: "My God, what is a heart?" Herbert asks. He wonders why God would eye our hearts and woo us. His questions to God are like the ones we ask: "Why, God, would you seek us out and shower your love on us? Why would you spend time so generously with each one of us?"[3]

George Herbert's thoughts still ring true. Why should the all-powerful God who rules the universe go to the trouble of pouring out his love to each person? In fact, we don't fully understand why God wants to express his love to us in prayer; yet this idea about how

God deals with us is not new. Such has been the long experience and tradition of Jewish and Christian faith—of Catholic faith.

DEVELOPING AN INNER DISPOSITION

While it is good to learn the many styles of Christian prayer and devotion, the real point of the spiritual life is developing an inner disposition: the continuing conversion and transformation of the heart. This was part of what Jesus constantly taught. Prayer is never a matter of externals, of lip service, or going through the motions. Instead, we want to open ourselves up to God's love and allow that love to set us on fire.

Throughout Christian and Catholic history we have many fine examples of this kind of deep and intentional prayer. And we can see from these examples how prayer has the power to light us up, to change us, to make us genuine disciples.

WHAT HOLDS US BACK?

In some ways prayer is attractive. At the same time we seem to resist it. Certain ingrained attitudes get in our way.

First of all, there's a language and philosophy of achievement that makes us think prayer is beside the point; a formality; something for those who are out of the mainstream and don't know what life is all about.

Second, a mentality of sophistication takes over. This mentality says unbelief is sophisticated and cool; belief is primitive and outmoded and belongs to another place and time.

Third, we may be caught up in a success-driven concept of space and time. We wonder what prayer will do for us. Such a conquest mentality doesn't leave much space for God.

Fourth, we fall prey to stereotypes. We think of prayer as rote performance or lip service. We're tripped up by a false and shallow understanding of prayer.

And fifth, we're sometimes discouraged because we don't often see people who are really practicing the life of prayer.

EXCUSES WE GIVE OURSELVES

Besides the obstacles just mentioned—most of which are cultural—there are also discouragements from within. Some of these are fairly common.

For one thing, there is the argument about time. *"I would pray, but I can't find the time."*

Secondly, there is low self-esteem that says, *"God talks to other people, not to me."*

A variation of this runs something like: *"Nothing will happen if I pray."* This particular problem stems, I think, from expecting large and bold results, like the parting of the Red Sea.

Some who are already very active in their churches think they are already doing enough for God. *"God knows how much I'm doing; therefore I don't need to pray."*

Most people who attempt a life of prayer have to deal with one or more of these. Excuses like these are really a nuisance, because they keep cropping up.

At the same time, they're like weeds in the garden; they can be dealt with. Though persistent, they are fairly superficial.

Sometimes our reluctance to pray goes deeper. We are afraid to pray because we are afraid of getting involved. We are less afraid of the prayer in which nothing happens than the prayer in which something happens.

A PRAYING ATTITUDE

One of my favorite examples of prayer takes place in a film classic most of us have seen many times.

It's about a man named George Bailey, who ran the Building & Loan in Bedford Falls after his father died. The film is by Frank Capra and explores the character of George Bailey (played by Jimmy Stewart) who is a good-hearted, ordinary person overwhelmed by the demands of living.

George has a series of confrontations with a really rotten power broker in his town, a man named Potter. Every time he has to deal with Potter, George always seizes the moral high ground. But inwardly he resents the way his life is going, and the personal sacrifices he has to make.

Finally he comes to a point of complete despair. He is ready to jump off a bridge—because the voices of desolation have convinced him he is worth more dead than alive.

Just before he does this, however, he prays. It is not a very confident prayer. It is not a very disciplined prayer. The style of it is: "If you're out there, if anybody's listening . . . if you can hear me. . . ." On a snowy Christmas Eve in a small American town, George Bailey sits on a barstool and addresses the God who is his last hope. "Father in heaven, I'm not a praying man, but if you're up there and you can hear me, show me the way. I'm at the end of my rope. Show me the way."

A few minutes later he is attacked by a vengeful customer, and regrets his prayer almost at once. "That's what I got for praying." It's clear that George Bailey is a pretty hopeless case when it comes to the spiritual life.

George Bailey's prayer—not formal, but heartfelt—is a very good kind of prayer. In this kind of prayer we lay our defenses down; we stop trying to be God for ourselves. When we give up, when we are exhausted, when we stop struggling, we allow God to be God, to surround us with the love we think we don't deserve.

It could be said that Frank Capra's film, *It's a Wonderful Life*, is a fable. It is a kind of fairy tale. Yet the way this film dramatizes George Bailey's prayer is quite realistic. Sometimes in our lives we come to moments when we don't know how to go on. We feel a need for God's support and love, but we are full of doubt and low self-esteem; we even feel unqualified to pray.

LETTING OUR DEFENSES DOWN

This prayer of inadequacy is very good prayer. It is honest, unvarnished. When we feel that we can't handle situations on our own, we are strengthened by turning to God, placing ourselves in God's hands.

Jesus tells the story of the tax collector and the Pharisee, who approach prayer in strikingly different ways. The Pharisee feels very qualified to pray. He is an expert, accomplished at prayer. He wants to show off about his righteousness. "God, I thank you that I am not like other people," says the Pharisee. He feels superior to the crowd of thieves, rogues, adulterers, and others who crowd into the Temple to pray. He definitely thinks he outranks the tax collector standing some distance away. The tax collector, on the other hand, feels very unqualified, very unworthy. He has little standing in the community, and he feels embarrassed to pray. "But the tax collector, standing far off, would not even look up to heaven, but was beating his breast and saying, 'God, be merciful to me, a sinner!'" (Lk. 18:10–13) Yet God hears his prayer; the tax collector's humility stands him in good stead. And Jesus explains that the tax collector went away "justified."

Both George Bailey and the tax collector have something to teach us about prayer. Prayer is not a skill or an achievement. Instead, it flows from a simple heart and a sincere desire to trust in God. Letting our defenses down is vital to any relationship of love.

PUT YOURSELF IN THE PRESENCE OF GOD

Over the centuries, this simple advice has been given for those who want to pray: "Put yourself in the presence of God." Right away we raise questions. Do we have to place ourselves in God's presence? Isn't God already here? It is true that, according to Christian belief, God is everywhere, already present before we call on him. In Isaiah 65 we read: "Before they call I will answer; and while they are yet speaking I will hear."

Even so, we need to put ourselves in the presence of a God who is already present. We make an interior action that allows us to sense that we are in the presence of God. God is seeking us out; but we have to cross the distance. It is an act of the will, of the baptized imagination, an act of faith. In one simple stroke we come into the presence of God. This fundamental decision, to come close to God, to speak to God, is the beginning of prayer. And in another sense it is prayer. In that new space (where is it? within ourselves? on some transcendent plane?)—no matter where, we reach an intersection between God and us. Now we are ready to speak to God and let God speak to us.

HOW DO I KNOW I'M REALLY PRAYING?

Sometimes we doubt our own ability to pray. We have heard that prayer is just a matter of entering the presence of God. But how do we know when we are really praying? Familiar with Bible stories in which manna falls in the desert, we may look for overt signs that God is really listening and willing to provide answers to our prayer.

Remembering his college days, Thomas Merton wrote of friends who wanted a relationship with God, but were waiting for a jolt, a lightning bolt of intervention. Without broad strokes of validation, they were hard put to believe that God was paying them any attention.

Trust is the first and possibly the most important attitude we should bring to prayer. If we don't see signs as big as lightning bolts, we should believe that God doesn't always need bold gestures to communicate with us. If we don't hear anything, or feel anything, we can still be confident that God is really there, really listening to us as we pray. We should not be too hard on God. We should not be too hard on ourselves. We should wait, settle down, be patient, and know that God wants us to pray, cares about our prayer, and is listening for what we have to say.

"Be still and know that I am God" (Ps. 46:10) is one of the best sayings in the Bible. As in any real friendship, conversation with God may develop slowly, with interruptions and silences. Accept God's ways.

Do not try to impose your expectations on God. Above all, do not be discouraged. Learn to accept and understand your own personality in prayer. Just as you believe in God, you must also believe in yourself as a person God loves and wants to know in prayer.

GOD, SO QUICKLY

Keep in mind that God speaks to us in very simple and ordinary ways: a phone call from a friend on a lackluster day, an unexpected visit, a break in the weather, a sudden shower of rain, a job offer. Even a life crisis can and should be interpreted in the light of grace. When moments of enlightenment come, we can thank God for them. Or, if we choose, we can say, rebelliously, "God had nothing to do with it!" Even the smallest blessing can make a theology. Rather than debate the possibility that God walks with us daily, we can accept God's presence, and thrive on what that friendship brings to our daily lives.

In Tennessee Williams's well-known play, *A Streetcar Named Desire*, one of the characters, Blanche, discovers that she is loved by a man named Mitch. Overcome with feeling, she says: "Sometimes there's God, so quickly!"

MANY MOODS OF PRAYER

In short, prayer is the way we pursue a relationship with the God who made us and wants us to come close. This is no casual acquaintance, but a friendship that will change and develop over time. Paul the Apostle speaks of the "depth and the riches and the wisdom and knowledge of God" (Rom. 11:33); he writes to the Ephesians about the "boundless riches of Christ." (Eph. 3:8) An inexhaustible treasure is waiting for us when we pursue the Christian life.

There are many moods of prayer, all part of deeper spiritual development. Let me suggest some of these moods.

God calls us to begin and we make the gift of ourselves, an ongoing surrender to the life of grace. So one phase, usually the first, is **beginning**. In fact, we may have to make many new beginnings over a lifetime of prayer.

God shows love to us in new and surprising ways; we yield to new and better understandings of the Divine Being. This second phase may be called **yielding**.

Sometimes within a life of devotion we come into times of dryness, times of desolation and trial; we are called upon to trust in God and wait patiently for a later time of consolation and enlightenment. This phase is often called **darkness**.

As we continue in the life of prayer, we begin to develop new ways of seeing, and the world itself, daily events and people, become more transparent to us. This phase may be called **transparency**.

As our prayer becomes more committed and intense we are sometimes called to new heights, to extremes of sacrificial love. This too is a common phase of prayer. I call it **fear of heights**, a reluctance to accept God's higher call, rather like what Moses and other prophets felt when assigned to do amazing things.

Spiritual friendship, not unlike the deep affection of Paul and Timothy, is part and parcel of spiritual life. I call it by Shakespeare's phrase, **hoops of steel**. One of his characters in *Hamlet* says, "Those friends thou hast and their adoption tried, grapple them to thy soul with hoops of steel." The expression suggests the binding power of God's grace and favor, and the deep attachments that grow up among those who are blessed by God's love.

Finally, my favorite term for intimacy with God is **clinging**, a term the Hebrew mystics use to suggest the closeness of God to us. We find this clinging mentioned in the Psalms. May we also find it in our own hearts.

MAPPING THE SPIRITUAL JOURNEY

One common phrase used today for the life of prayer is "the spiritual journey." The seven moods just mentioned might be considered as a road map for the journey that begins when prayer is no longer a random activity, but an ongoing discovery, an adventure. Beginning is a kind of homecoming or return to God, a little act of repentance like that of the Prodigal Son. Even if you haven't been away from God entirely, your decision to pray is a new gift of yourself, a deeper commitment to be present to God.

Yielding is another term for surrender. This language may strike you as romantic. Yet many spiritual writers describe this process in an unromantic way. C. S. Lewis says that his conversion felt rather ordinary. "There was no strain of music from within . . . no smell of eternal orchards at the threshold, when I was dragged through the doorway."[4] In another account, Lewis mentions that when God got through to him at last he seemed to hear the Lord saying, "Put down your gun and we'll talk." The language was drawn from Western movies![5]

About darkness: many people have experienced times of dryness or trial. Spiritual teachers usually consider this a necessary passage in the spiritual life. Thomas Merton has written: "What you most need in this dark journey is an unfaltering trust in the divine guidance, as well as the courage to risk everything for Him."[6]

Ignatius Loyola speaks less of darkness than of desolation. He points out that the spiritual life will include times of desolation followed by times of consolation. This alternating to-and-fro is to be expected. Another Jesuit writer, Jean Pierre de Caussade, assures us that in spite of such ups and downs, God is always to be found in the moment. De Caussade writes: "The present moment always reveals the presence and the power of God. Every moment we live through is like an ambassador who declares the will of God, and our hearts always utter their acceptance."[7] Whether we realize it or not, he explains, we are moving forward in our journey toward God.

Where spiritual friendship is concerned, there are many examples in Scripture and in the lives of the saints. Look forward to this gift in your own spiritual life, as you come to share your prayer experiences with spiritual directors and trusted friends. Paul writes to Timothy: "Night and day, I thank God . . . and always I remember you in my prayers; I remember your tears and long to see you again to complete my happiness. . . . This is why I am reminding you now to fan into a flame the gift that God gave you when I laid my hands on you." (2 Tim. 1:3–4, 6–7)

Union, or the unitive life, is considered the fullness of the spiritual life. Of this union C. S. Lewis has said just a little, all the while protesting that he is "not the one to speak."

Lewis says: "All that can be said here is that even on those high levels, though something goes from man to God, yet all, including this something, comes from God to man. If he rises, he does so lifted on the wave of the incoming tide of God's love for him. He becomes nothing in that ascension. His love is perfected by becoming, in a sense, nothing. He is less than a mote in that sunbeam, vanishes, not from God's sight, but from ours and his own, into the nuptial solitude of the love that loves love, and in love, all things."[8]

A FEW FUNDAMENTALS

For most of us a prayer life means structure. It need not be rigid or inflexible structure, but a daily or weekly schedule for prayer and spiritual reading is a good idea. When we plan, when we establish good habits, creativity comes into play. Prayer life should be designed to suit one's own needs and tastes, and to fit more or less comfortably within other commitments. For this reason, the schedule should not be too ambitious.

Questions arise. Do I need a certain space? A special church? A particular chair? Countless recipes exist for prayerfulness. Some like to pray in a garden. Some prefer a city park. Some choose a place in their own homes and make it a sacred space for prayer. Some who are on the run bring along a notebook, a Bible, a few pages of sacred text, as the "construction paper" for an inner temple, a temple of the heart. Some are nurtured by silence, the great silences of cathedrals (actually they can be noisy places as tourists and other worshippers trundle about) or the small silences of retreat houses and country places. Others learn to pray against the white noise of cities, against the sound of engines revving as planes taxi forth for takeoff. In the middle of the whirlwind is a little voice, God's voice, saying, "I Am." My guess is that, in a well-planned prayer life, there will be some novelty and some routine. The routine and the novelty become our context for prayer.

If our lives are scattered and driven by stress, we may even be praying to have a routine, to arrive at some predictability and evenness in what we do. We hope prayer will stabilize and center us. Others may feel, *my life is too much the same old thing.* For them, prayer can provide newness, refreshment, even a kind of drama, a heightened awareness of things as they are.

In short, the structure of our spiritual lives is simply a framework for prayer. Spontaneous, creative praying transcends the structure. When you really begin to practice the life of prayer and devotion, everything works together.

EXAMINING ONE'S HEART

It is a good idea to examine one's heart often, and on a regular schedule. Set aside a certain time each week for an examination of conscience, or as it is sometimes called, an examination of consciousness.

Consider the many blessings you have had since the last time you did this exercise. Take stock of the many ways that God has protected you and made his presence known in your life. Then take stock of the ways you may have fallen short of the grace of God.

If there is a sinful pattern in your life, resolve to overcome it. Make a firm purpose to amend your life. Consider frequent reception of the sacraments (Eucharist and Reconciliation) as a way to grow in virtue and holiness.[9]

ASKING AND RECEIVING

Jesus recommends that we ask the Father for whatever we need; he assures us that the Father will respond. "But if God so clothes the grass of the field, which is alive today and tomorrow is thrown into the oven, will he not much more clothe you—you of little faith?" (Mt. 6:30)

Sometimes we ask for our own needs. That is called prayer of petition. When we ask in behalf of others, we call it prayer of intercession. Some speak of "lifting up" their friends and loved ones in prayer.

But beyond the prayer of asking comes the prayer of receiving. This prayer, of simply resting in God, being with the Lord, conversing with him, sharing in his friendship, becoming united to God, is a form of contemplation. When you feel such an impulse, give way to it. The best modern teachers of prayer assure us that contemplation is for everyone. As you become a person of prayer, you may begin to find your contemplative side. Contemplation is considered the highest form of prayer, but all forms of prayer are excellent and valuable.

WHAT IF GOD DOESN'T GIVE US WHAT WE ASK FOR?

This is one of the most frequent questions voiced about prayer. It seems that everything Jesus says to us encourages us to think that if we pray rightly, God will answer our prayer. Jesus assures us that God is a loving father who will provide for all our needs.

When we don't get what we pray for, we question ourselves. Did I ask for something I'm not supposed to have? Should I have prayed longer, or harder? Is God trying to tell me something by not giving me what I request?

Many have prayed fervently for a beloved person who is sick to get well again, or for a person to be spared from death. When such prayers (and smaller requests) are not granted, the person of faith must accept the answer—what seems like a non-answer—in faith and trust.

Faith requires that we accept God's wisdom as greater than our own.

In the spiritual life, trusting God's decisions when we don't understand them is called by various names: acceptance, submission, obedience. Unanswered prayers can become opportunities for grace.

A WORD ABOUT INTENSITY

One aspect of Catholic prayer is that it is, or can become, somewhat intense, according to the personality and the devotion of the one who prays (and the graces received). Catholic prayer seems designed to allow and sanction this intensity. There are many examples among the lives of the saints of the inner transformation that can take place through such an intense relationship to God. For some of us this intensity is expressed outwardly, in charismatic and enthusiastic ways. But historically, Catholic prayer has often been a matter of inwardness and depth. This wide range of devotional styles is part of the treasure box of Catholic spiritual life.

NOTES

1. Emily Dickinson, "Prayer is the little implement," in Roger Lundin, *Emily Dickinson and the Art of Belief* (Grand Rapids, Mich.: Eerdmans, 1998), 146.
2. George Herbert, "Prayer (I)," in *The Works of George Herbert*, ed. F. E. Hutchinson (Oxford: Clarendon Press, 1945), 51. Spelling and punctuation modernized.
3. Herbert, "Mattens," *The Works of George Herbert*, 62.
4. C. S. Lewis, *Surprised by Joy: The Shape of My Early Life* (London: Geoffrey Bles, 1955), 217.
5. C. S. Lewis, *God in the Dock: Essays on Theology and Ethics*, ed. Walter Hooper (Grand Rapids, Mich.: Eerdmans, 1970), 261.
6. Thomas Merton, *New Seeds of Contemplation* (New York: New Directions, 1961), 243.
7. Jean Pierre de Caussade, *Abandonment to Divine Providence* (New York: Doubleday Image Books, 1975), 50.

8. C. S. Lewis, "Agape," in audio recording, *Four Talks on Love* (Atlanta, Ga.: The Episcopal Radio TV Foundation, n.d.).
9. Note that the prayer of examen is explained more completely in the section, "Prayer and the Virtuous Life," chapter 9.

Becoming Intentional

GOD IN THREE PERSONS:
MAKING THE SIGN OF THE CROSS

Take for example the Sign of the Cross, one of the commonest of our prayers. We make the Sign of the Cross as an entranceway to many sacred actions. First we touch the forehead; second, the breast; third, the left shoulder; and fourth, the right shoulder. (Among Orthodox Christians this sign is made somewhat differently; but in Roman, Anglican, and Orthodox Catholic churches the spirit and form of the prayer are very much the same.) We say: "In the name of the Father, and of the Son, and of the Holy Spirit. Amen."

This prayer, which is ingrained and familiar, can be done almost mindlessly or automatically; or it can be done attentively and devotedly. The best way is to speak these words (and make the accompanying sign) very intentionally, so that the prayer opens us up to the central mystery of our faith: our God is one God in Three Persons. Possibly at some time we have tried to grapple with the theological meaning of the Trinity; we have tried to consider the mysterious core of this teaching. Maybe we have found this central core of teaching difficult, even baffling. No matter. When we make the Sign of the Cross we are not thinking about doctrine. Instead, we are opening ourselves to a deeper faith level, the mystery of the triune God. This opening up is central to our prayer. Prayer is intention, a reaching, a stretching toward the desired Other, coming into the heart of God, the Beloved.

One of the best things about this prayer is its ancientness. Christians have been voicing this prayer and using this sign for a very long time. Whenever we say this prayer we join ourselves not only to God, but to the nameless Christians who have used this prayer throughout the centuries. We align ourselves with the Communion of Saints.

With this prayer we also appropriate the Cross of Christ. We take the Gospel words, the saying of Jesus, and plant them in our hearts: "If any want to become my followers, let them deny themselves and take up their cross daily and follow me." (Lk. 9:23) In crossing ourselves (as the common expression has it) we take upon ourselves the mystery of the Cross:

"Take my yoke upon you and learn from me. . . .
For my yoke is easy and my burden is light."
(Mt. 11:29, 30)

ADDRESSING THE FATHER:
THE OUR FATHER

Much traditional prayer follows the same pattern as the
Sign of the Cross. We address ourselves to God the
Father, through God the Son, in God the Holy Spirit.
It is Trinitarian prayer. Sometimes we find it hard to
imagine the three Divine Persons of the Trinity in relationship to each other and to us. But many ancient
prayers lead us from one Person to Another in a simple sequence.

One clear precedent for addressing God the Father
comes from Jesus himself. His disciples asked him how
to pray, and he responded with the words of the prayer
we know as the Our Father, or the Lord's Prayer.

Usually in Catholic churches we recite this prayer
in the following words:

> Our Father, who art in heaven,
> Hallowed be thy name;
> Thy kingdom come; thy will be done;
> On earth as it is in heaven.
> Give us this day our daily bread;
> And forgive us our trespasses
> As we forgive those who trespass against us.

And lead us not into temptation
But deliver us from evil.
(See Mt. 6:9–13)

In many churches the following words (which do not appear in the Gospel version) are added: "For thine is the kingdom, and the power, and the glory, forever and ever." Within the Roman Catholic Mass, these words are added (after some intervening text): "For the kingdom, the power, and the glory are yours, now and forever. Amen."

Contemporary people are mostly used to the idea of addressing God as Father. But this was not usual in the ancient world. So Jesus is breaking new ground when he teaches his disciples to pray, "Our Father." Also, Jesus uses and teaches a very familiar way of speaking to God, addressing God as *Abba*, a sort of in-the-family name for father, something like "Daddy" or "Papa." Paul the apostle in his preaching continues to address God in this familiar way, *Abba*, Father.

Every Christian is expected to know the Lord's Prayer by heart. Still, we should take care to honor this prayer by saying it very attentively and with full intention. When saying the prayer with a group, the pace is usually set by whoever is leading the prayer. But in private we may use the Our Father in a way that lets us savor the sacredness of this prayer. We may slow the prayer down, pausing for reflective silence at the end of each phrase. When we imagine God as Father we may call to mind that tender description in Hosea in which God speaks as a loving parent: "I was to them like those/who lift infants to their cheeks/I bent down to them and fed them."(Hosea 11:4)

EUCHARISTIC PRAYERS:
EUCHARIST AS PRAYER

Whenever we take part in Eucharist we notice that the Eucharistic prayers are addressed to God the Father in a way that invites us deeply into prayer. This prayer is said by the priest or bishop who is celebrating the Mass. Of course, he recites this prayer for all who are present (and for many others as well).

Catholics who attend Mass frequently may find that they know some prayers of the Mass by heart, without having tried to memorize them. This kind of memorizing, which comes almost as second nature, is all to the good. Many phrases are hidden deep in our hearts and may come to mind, not just at church, but at other times of the day or week.

> Father, you are holy indeed
> And all creation rightly gives you praise.

While we are attending Mass, this first phrase of the Eucharistic prayer invites everyone present into deeper reverence and adoration. When the prayer begins the whole congregation kneels. There is a rustling, a sound of pew-kneelers going into place, a hush that calls us to devotion.

The Eucharistic prayer places God (Father, Son, and Holy Spirit) before us in a vivid way:

> All life, all holiness comes from you
> through your Son, Jesus Christ our Lord,
> by the working of the Holy Spirit.

The Eucharistic prayers also have a way of telling us the faith-story again:

> From age to age you gather a people to yourself
> So that from east to west
> a perfect offering may be made
> to the glory of your name.

Whether we attend Mass daily, or weekly, we can learn to pray the Mass, not just by listening, but also by taking full part, by giving ourselves intentionally to the ongoing, on-flowing prayers. The structure of the Mass is always the same, but we notice variations from week to week and season to season, different readings, different feasts, different Gospels. Yet the Mass always maintains for us a sacred environment in which God can pour out his love and we can express our devotion in return.

PRAYING THE PREFACES

As the year goes along, and we faithfully take part in the Eucharist, certain other prayers in the Mass may enter our hearts and become part of our own private prayer. I particularly love this part of one of the Easter prefaces, and I sometimes use it as part of my prayer, whether or not we are in the Easter season. It refers to the saving action of Jesus Christ.

> In him a new age has dawned,
> the long reign of sin is ended;
> a broken world has been renewed,
> and man is once again made whole.

PRAYING THE PSALMS

One of the best, most ancient ways of praying is to use the psalms as prayer. Biblical Psalms are an assembled group of prayers, meant to be used both privately and in congregations. This is the ancient prayer of the Hebrew people. It is also the prayer book that Jesus used.

The psalms become familiar to us when we read them over in a prayerful spirit and with deep intention. You may have a system or plan; but you don't need a system to do this. Just browse through the psalms in your Bible, choosing one that appeals to you. Then make that psalm your prayer for a while—five or fifteen minutes, or longer if your time permits. Join your intention to that of the Psalmist.

Maybe one or more of the psalms appeals to you so much that you want to learn the text by heart. That is a wonderful thing to do, for you are carrying the prayer in memory with you wherever you are. Psalm 23, "The Lord is my shepherd," is a favorite. So is Psalm 91, often considered a prayer of protection: "You who live in the shelter of the Most High/who abide in the shadow of the Almighty." (Ps. 91:1–2) When you are in a tight spot and feel the need to pray, you may inwardly recite some phrases from a psalm you know by heart.

Psalms express a very wide range of moods. Psalm 130 is a psalm of deep need and lament: "Out of the depths I cry to you, O Lord/Lord, hear my voice." This psalm is often called by its Latin name, the "De Profundis," a phrase meaning "out of the depths." A number of psalms and canticles, used often for prayer, are well known by their Latin names.

When Jesus prayed from the Cross, his words were, "My God, My God, why have you forsaken me?" (Mt. 27:46) We can assume that these words of Psalm 22 came spontaneously to his lips when he was under severe duress. Even within such psalms of lament, voicing difficulty and distress, there are also words of consolation and reassurance to fortify us in dark times.

THE LITURGY OF THE HOURS

In monasteries, convents, and houses of prayer, the psalms are prayed at different times of day, throughout the twenty-four hours. This arrangement of the psalms for daily use is known as the Liturgy of the Hours.

Priests, brothers, and sisters use this liturgy as part of their daily commitment to prayer. Some laypeople use it too. This system of prayer has developed over time, and much of it is a matter of custom. To develop skill and confidence in using these prayers, you may need some instruction—say, at a retreat house—from someone, like a sister, who uses these prayers daily.

Recently, when I was leading a weekend retreat at a retreat center not far from my home, we took part in Morning Prayer, led by a laywoman who is forming a new religious community with the approval of her local bishop. She is enthusiastic and experienced in praying and leading the Liturgy of the Hours, and was able to teach us how to pray it gracefully.

The liturgical customs attached to this kind of prayer are beautiful. For instance, certain psalms are prayed antiphonally—one side of the congregation prays, then the other side responds. The rhythm of the praying is matched by the beauty of the psalms themselves. Also a kind of freshness, along with depth of intention, may spring up among those who are praying.

SAMPLE TEXTS

The Lord's Prayer,
also called the Our Father

Our Father, who art in heaven,
Hallowed be thy name;
Thy kingdom come; thy will be done;
On earth as it is in heaven.
Give us this day our daily bread;
And forgive us our trespasses
As we forgive those who trespass against us.
And lead us not into temptation
But deliver us from evil. Amen.

Sample Preface (Easter IV)

Father, all-powerful and ever-living God,
we do well always and everywhere to give you thanks
through Jesus Christ our Lord.
We praise you with greater joy than ever in this
Easter season,
when Christ became our paschal sacrifice.
In him a new age has dawned,
the long reign of sin is ended;
a broken world has been renewed,
and man is once again made whole.
The joy of the resurrection renews the whole world,
while the choirs of heaven sing forever to your glory.

Sample Eucharistic Prayer
(from Eucharistic Prayer IV)

Father in Heaven,
it is right that we should give you thanks and glory:
you are the one God, living and true.
Through all eternity you live in unapproachable
    light.
Source of all life and goodness, you have created all
    things
to fill your creatures with every blessing
and lead all men to the joyful vision of your light.
Countless hosts of angels stand before you to do
    your will;
they look upon your splendor
and praise you, night and day.
United with them,
and in the name of every creature under heaven,
we too praise your glory as we say:

Holy, holy, holy Lord, God of power and might,
heaven and earth are full of your glory,
    Hosanna in the highest.
Blessed is he who comes in the name of the Lord.
    Hosanna in the highest.

Excerpt from Morning Prayer

In the name of the Father, and of the Son, and of the
Holy Spirit.
Amen.
God, come to my assistance. Lord, make haste to
help me.
Glory be to the Father, and to the Son, and to the
Holy Spirit.
As it was in the beginning, is now, and ever shall be,
world without end,
Amen.[1]

Hymn

Glory in the heights to the Lord,
on earth peace,
to us favor.
We praise you,
bless you,
worship you,
laud you,
we give you thanks,
for your greatest glory,
O Lord, king of heaven,
God the Father all-powerful,
Lord the only Son,
Jesus Christ,
and you, Holy Spirit.

O Lord God,
God's Lamb,
the Father's Son,
you take the world's sins away:
have mercy on us.
you take the world's sins away:
accept our prayer.
you sit at the Father's right hand:
have mercy on us.
For you alone are holy,
you alone are Lord,
O Jesus Christ
for God the Father's glory.
Amen.

NOTE

1. Excerpt, adapted from "Morning Prayer," as given in Terence Cardinal Cooke, *Prayers for Today* (New York: Macmillan, 1971), 167–68.

Visiting with Christ Jesus

CHRIST-CENTERED PRAYER: EUCHARISTIC ADORATION

There are many forms of Christ-centered prayer in the Catholic tradition. One of the most moving and life-transforming is prayer honoring the Real Presence, that is, the presence of Jesus Christ in the consecrated elements of bread and wine. These consecrated elements of bread and wine are often referred to as the Blessed Sacrament. Catholics believe that Christ is fully present in either one of the consecrated elements of bread and wine. They are no longer bread and wine but the Body and Blood of Christ.

In Catholic custom the consecrated wafer is often reserved, or set aside, for prayer, sometimes on a side altar in a large church, sometimes in a chapel dedicated for this purpose. When you enter a church you can determine where the sacrament is reserved. You will find that a sanctuary lamp is lighted near the tabernacle. In religious houses, communities of priests, sisters, or brothers, it is usual to find a room set aside for Eucharistic adoration, that is, prayer focused upon Jesus in the Blessed Sacrament.

There is no required format for praying in front of the Blessed Sacrament. However, extreme reverence is expected. Upon entering a chapel where the Blessed Sacrament is reserved, it is customary to genuflect—bend the right knee to the ground, prayerfully, possibly also making the sign of the cross.

On special occasions the Blessed Sacrament is exposed for devotion, usually in a vessel called a monstrance.[1] Monstrance is a term that comes from the Latin word meaning "to show." A monstrance is a vessel for showing the Blessed Sacrament to the faithful. When this happens, a double genuflection is expected: upon entering the presence of the exposed Sacrament, the faithful person kneels briefly, with both knees touching the ground.

These practices reflect the belief that Jesus is especially present for our adoration in this place, at this time. All prayer is based on the belief that God is present to us, that we can enter God's presence. But for believers, the Lord's real presence in the Eucharist is a powerful invitation to prayer and devotion.

Over time, certain ways of praying in front of the Blessed Sacrament have been developed. There are rituals for making what is known as a Holy Hour. Benediction is a special religious service that takes place when the Blessed Sacrament is exposed for devotion.

But praying to Jesus in the Blessed Sacrament can also be very spontaneous and informal. That is, we are outwardly silent and reverential. But inwardly, we speak to the Lord very intimately and personally about whatever is on our hearts. And we listen. We let the Lord speak to us, by waiting for the Lord's word and voice to us.

Much has been written about this kind of simple prayer. One of the books that nourished me in this kind of devotion is by the English convert and writer, Ronald Knox. His book about Eucharistic devotion is called *The Window in the Wall*. The window, of course, is the circular form of the consecrated host. As we focus our heart-prayer intensely upon this "window" we are able to enter into the presence of God, to break through the "wall" that seemingly separates the human from the divine.

THE WINDOW IN THE WALL

Knox develops this idea by saying we ourselves have put up the wall between us and God. It is a wall of sense and of pride, the wall we built by disobedience. "Our wall—we raised it against God, not he against us; we raised it, when Adam sinned, and when each of us took up again the legacy of sinfulness in his own life." But Christ, through his Incarnation and Passion,

has made a great window. Knox attributes this idea to
St. Paul: "he made both one, breaking down the wall
that was a barrier between us," just as the Temple veil
was torn in two. The passage Knox is referring to is
Ephesians 2:11–14, in which Paul speaks of how the
Gentiles have been brought into salvation by the cross
of Christ. "He has broken down the dividing wall,"
Paul writes. But Knox applies this breaking down of
walls to Christ breaking through to us in prayer.

Knox continues: "the window is there for all time,
if we would only recognize it." Christ himself, in his
risen and glorified body, is the window between two
worlds. Knox describes the sacred host as a "glittering
disc of whiteness . . . not reflecting the light of the candles in front of it, but . . . penetrated with a light of its
own, a light not of this world, shining through it from
behind, as if through a window, outdazzling gold and
candle-flame with a more intense radiance." Is this just
a trick of the eye, an impression we receive because of
our devotion? Knox says it is not an illusion but a
glimpse of the truth of God's presence among us.[2]

PRAISING GOD IN THE BLESSED SACRAMENT

Many prayers and hymns have been written to praise
God in the Blessed Sacrament. One of these, a Latin
hymn, attributed to St. Thomas Aquinas, is called
"Adoro Te Devote," which in English may be rendered, "I Adore You Devotedly." In my early days as
a Roman Catholic I wrote a translation of that hymn.

Here are a few stanzas. The entire translation is given at the end of this chapter.

From the Latin Hymn "Adoro Te Devote," Ascribed to Saint Thomas Aquinas

> I adore You, God in hiding,
> You in other shapes abiding,
> My whole heart bows meek and low,
> Knowing You has made it so.
>
> —
>
> Sight and touch and taste betray;
> Only hearing shows the way;
> God's Son speaks and I believe;
> God's own Truth cannot deceive.
>
> —
>
> God so hid upon the cross
> Even His manhood seemed a loss;
> I confess Him God; and pray
> With the thief who died that day.
>
> —
>
> Thomas saw the wounds and knew;
> I see not, yet say to You,
> "God and Lord!" Pray, make me move
> More toward hope in You and love.

One of the most remarkable times for Eucharistic devotion in the Christian year is on Holy Thursday. It is traditional, at the end of the Holy Thursday service, to carry the Blessed Sacrament in procession throughout the church, up one aisle and down another, singing a beautiful Latin hymn called "Pange Lingua" ("Sing, My Tongue"). This hymn is an ancient melody that evokes the awe and wonder of centuries-old Christian devotion. As the ministers pass through the congregation, the faithful who are present kneel to express their reverence. Finally the Blessed Sacrament reaches a side altar or special chapel where it is kept until midnight for the adoration of those present in the church. At midnight, when Good Friday begins, the Blessed Sacrament is taken away.

THE SACRED HEART

Devotion to the Sacred Heart of Jesus has been a distinctively Catholic way of praying for centuries. It may date back as far as the year 1000; but the Sacred Heart devotion we know today was strongly influenced by particular revelations to St. Mary Margaret Alacoque, a seventeenth-century religious. Private revelations were given to her: appearances of Jesus the Lord at Paray-le-Mondial in the years 1673–1675. The Sacred Heart devotion antedated her visions. But as her visions became widely known, they influenced the Sacred Heart devotion. The most common representation of the Sacred Heart of Jesus shows him with a bright red Valentine-shaped heart, bleeding, to indicate the intensity of his love for us and his sorrow for the world.[3]

In earlier times Catholics concentrated on the physical heart of Jesus. In those days the physical heart was thought to be the seat of the emotions. Modern Catholic interpreters now link the Sacred Heart devotion to scriptural sources in which the heart is taken to mean the whole inner life. In this way, many references to the heart in the Psalms (Ps. 15:9, 21:15, 39:7–9, and 68:21) and in Jeremiah, especially Jeremiah 3:21, may be applied to the Sacred Heart devotion.

Today, Catholics connect with the depth of love expressed by the Sacred Heart of Jesus. Another aspect of the Sacred Heart is thought to be the virtue of Jesus. In using Sacred Heart prayer and devotion, we are seeking a virtue like that of Jesus. In short, when we express devotion to the Sacred Heart we are asking for God's love to flow into us. We are asking to become like Jesus in his heartfelt care.

> Deepen our faith
> and touch fire to our hearts
> that we may respond with love
> to the great love for us
> and for all men and women
> that fills your Sacred Heart.[4]

When I was becoming Catholic in my twenties I made my first retreat and discovered the power of this particular devotion. Later on, I came to see that this devotion does not belong to this or that religious community but to all the faithful.

Some spiritual writers seem to have been especially formed by devotion to the Sacred Heart. One of these is Pierre Teilhard de Chardin, who in his book, *The Divine Milieu* says this:

"I cleave to the creative power of God; I co-incide with it; I become not only its instrument but its living prolongation. And since there is nothing more personal in a being than its will, I merge myself, in a sense, through my heart, with the very heart of God. This contact is continuous because I am always acting."[5] A bit later on he refers to Christ as having a "blessed hold" on the universe. Christ is drawing all things to himself.

Of course, the devotion is central to certain religious communities (such as the Society of the Sacred Heart) but this devotion is by no means exclusive to them. When my daughters attended the Academy of the Sacred Heart in New Orleans, I became very fond of the lovely hymn sung by students, faculty, and friends of the school:

Coeur de Jésus sauvez le monde,
Que l'univers vous soit soumis,
En Vous seul notre espoir se fonde,
Seigneur, Seigneur, Vous nous l'avez promis[6]

Heart of Jesus, save the world;
May the universe submit to You;
In You alone we root our hope
Lord, Lord You promised it to us.

Vous l'avez dit, votre promesse.
Fait notre espoir, notre bonheur.
Je benirait dans ma tendresse,
Les enfants de Mon Sacré Coeur.

You said so Yourself, Your promise
Is our hope, our happiness.
Through my tenderness I will bless
The children of my Sacred Heart.

ICONS, IMAGES, AND STAINED GLASS

Not long ago a friend of mine who is Eastern Orthodox gave me an icon of Christ. I was touched by his gesture because our two branches of Christianity have been divided for a thousand years, yet we share some styles of devotion. The use of images (including icons) is an authentically Catholic (and simple) way to pray.

Many religious stores offer beautiful icons for sale. These are often rendered by artists who are working in a long tradition, replicating icons of Jesus (and others) from very early Christian sources. To own an icon (even a small one) is rather like having the Blessed Sacrament under one's own roof, usually a privilege for those in religious societies and institutions. Thomas Merton said in his autobiography, *The Seven Storey Mountain*, that he was drawn to live under the same roof as the Blessed Sacrament. Eventually that attraction drew him into religious life.

Another way to pray with icons is by using a book, like the one by Henri Nouwen, which provides reproductions of icons, along with personal reflections. The book I have in mind is *Behold the Beauty of the Lord: Praying with Icons.*[7] It reproduces the Icon of the Holy Trinity, the Icon of the Virgin of Vladimir, the Icon of the Savior of Zvenigorod, and the Icon of the Descent of the Holy Spirit. Nouwen offers a meditation on each one. You may read and pray with the author, until you want to move beyond his reflections, focusing entirely on the Lord. Christ may speak to you personally through this kind of encounter. Father Nouwen, in his text, speaks of having gazed upon these four icons until he memorized them as he had done with verbal prayers such as the Our Father and the Hail Mary. "An icon," he writes, "is like a window looking out upon eternity." Each time he returns to the icon (even if he already knows it by heart) he finds there is something new to be seen. The method of prayer he recommends is not thinking or reflecting or looking, but simply gazing. The gazing is a form of devotion, a very ancient and a very effective one.

One way that Jesus became very present to our ancestors was in the elaborate stained glass in churches and monasteries. These beautiful artifacts often show scenes in the life of Christ: Jesus walking on the waves, calming the storm, letting the little children come. Sometimes Christ is depicted as the Good Shepherd.

Part of the richness of Catholic devotion is in the use of such imagery. The religious imagination is happily evoked by sacred art and artifacts.

How do we pray with such images and artifacts?

We let the image help us to focus on God. We come to quiet and let the Lord speak to us in his unique way. We listen for God's voice and respond when the time comes.

Another commonplace devotional image of the Christ is a crucifix. The crucifix is dominant in Catholic churches and very common in Catholic schools, institutions, religious houses, and private homes. Every rosary is made with a crucifix. So Catholic believers are rarely lacking a crucifix of one kind or another to be used for personal devotion.

ST. FRANCIS OF ASSISI AND THE CRUCIFIX

An unusual incident took place when Francis of Assisi, a young man just discovering the inner life, went to pray in the broken-down church of San Damiano. This was not just a casual prayer. Francis was in the middle of a full-scale conversion of heart. While praying before a small Byzantine-style crucifix Francis heard the Lord say, "Go and repair my house, which you see is falling down." Francis obeyed this command on two levels. He renounced his worldly life in a radical way and took up a religious life of voluntary poverty, prayer, preaching, and service to the poor. Soon he had formed a band of poor preachers who traveled far in the service of Christ. Francis also saw to it that the church of San Damiano was repaired. Pilgrims still visit this church and see the crucifix that became the focus of Francis's encounter with Christ. But the zeal of the Franciscans also helped to repair the broader church, by renewing the vitality of spiritual life and dedicated Christian service.

SACRED WORKS OF ART

Works of art may become part of our devotions, especially if we seek out the best religious art available to us.

Recently in our small city of Alexandria, Louisiana, we were privileged to have a museum exhibit of more than a hundred Spanish artworks entitled *Heart of Spain*. Among the painters were El Greco, Goya, Velasquez, and Murillo. Because my husband and I had helped to write some of the accompanying audio material, we visited the exhibit four or five times. I had a fine chance to experience the artworks devotionally.

A number of these dealt with the Passion of Christ. There was a roomful of the Virgin Mary, ranging from the annunciation to the coronation of the Virgin in heaven. Four impressive paintings of archangels—large canvases—were displayed on either side of a great hall.

As often happens with an exhibit seen more than once, a certain painting became dominant for me. I felt that the painting spoke to me; it sought me out. Was this a movement of grace? I thought so.

In this particular painting, the Virgin—shown as a handsome Spanish woman of thirty or so—was dressed in a garment of queenly red and gold. Slightly above her, the three persons of the Trinity hovered, placing a heavenly crown on her head. The Son, to the left, was a young bearded man in a red robe. The Father, to the right, was an old white-bearded man in a dark garment. At the center, directly over the Virgin's crown, was the dove, representing the Spirit. This anonymous painting is thought to be from the circle of Jerónimo Jacinto Espinosa (1600–1667).

Reflecting on the exhibit, I saw it had presented me with two major Christian images: the cross and the crown.

We bought the *Heart of Spain* catalog in order to savor certain paintings again. Their devotional impact was remarkable.[8]

Here, as with the icons, the principal method of prayer is gazing. It is more than just looking or observing, but a deeply intentional way of being in God's presence through a sacred work of art. Father Nouwen reminds us that gazing is an aspect of contemplation.

For the purpose of prayer and devotion, I have a small collection of religious works of art on postcards and in books. My collection includes Salvador Dali's *John of the Cross* (a representation of the Crucifixion from above) and Stanley Spencer's *The Resurrection: Cookham.*

The Lord has many ways of dealing with us, and can communicate through non-religious paintings as well. Many other forms of art, such as music, dance, theater, and pageantry, can also deepen our devotion.

THE WAY OF THE CROSS

Meditating on the Passion and death of Jesus is a long-established simple way to pray. Veneration of the Cross is part of the Easter liturgy, of course, but the Way of the Cross is practiced any time of year. To encourage this devotion, most Catholic churches have representations of the Stations of the Cross. In small churches and large cathedrals, one may observe individuals and groups passing quietly from the first to the fourteenth or fifteenth station,[9] stopping at each one to pray, addressing Jesus each time:

Verse. We adore you, Christ, and we bless you.
Response: Because by your holy cross you have redeemed the world.

To enhance this experience of prayer, many written meditations and reflections have been composed. Books and pamphlets help to deepen our devotion. But it is not just a matter of reading what others feel and say. We must pour ourselves into an expression of love and gratitude for the sacrifice of the Savior.

Once I made the Stations of the Cross outdoors on the grounds of a Jesuit retreat house on Long Island. As I went from one station to the next, praying with my whole heart, not using set devotions, but improvising my prayer, I was deeply moved. I "gave myself" to the Lord once again, as I had done before, but now in a new way. I wrote this poem to capture that experience.

Stations of the Cross, Inisfada

At the first station
I promised to be yours completely.
By the fifth station
you swept me away.
At the twelfth station
I knew I had promised a dozen times over.
And at the fourteenth
I closed my eyes against the sun
and the cross burned red into my brain.

✛

I have given myself to you;
there is no turning back.
Yet something in me wants to run.
Even a little sharing of your cross
is more than I can bear.
The things you ask—hard things—
make me break into a terror of sweat.
I do not have the strength for Calvary.

✛

Let me tell the authorities I have changed
my mind!
Let me recant,
say I was making it all up,
a child's hoax,
a dalliance, a make-believe.
I cannot walk with you, my Lord.
Your stride is longer.

✛

Yet even as I think it
I feel the print of the nails in my hands
and I am filled with love.[10]

Leaflets, books, and pamphlets can help us to make the Stations of the Cross. The point of this devotion, however, is not to recite any certain set prayers, but rather to place yourself with the Lord Jesus in his time of trial. You might consider reading first, an account of the Passion in one of the four Gospels. (You will not find Veronica mentioned there by name, but long tradition has it that she wiped the face of Jesus with her veil.) Then, as you move from the first station to the fourteenth, place yourself in each scene with Jesus. The fifteenth station, "Jesus is Risen," is not always found. However, the Crucifixion and Resurrection are always linked in our devotion. Even when more emphasis is placed on the sufferings of Jesus, it is all in the context of his final victory over sin and death. The familiar verse and response can be used as a responsorial reading when a number of persons are making the stations together. If it is used for private prayer, the individual may read both verse and response at each station. A book that represents both the stations and the prayers (with illustrations) can be a helpful way to make the stations anywhere.

SAMPLE TEXTS

"Adoro Te Devote"

I adore You, God in hiding,
You in other shapes abiding,
My whole heart bows meek and low,
Knowing You has made it so.

Sight and touch and taste betray;
Only hearing shows the way;
God's Son speaks and I believe;
God's own Truth cannot deceive.

God so hid upon the cross
Even His manhood seemed a loss;
I confess Him God; and pray
With the thief who died that day.

Thomas saw the wounds and knew;
I see not, yet say to You,
"God and Lord!" Pray, make me move
More toward hope in You and love.

O reminder of God's death,
Living Bread that gives us breath,
Let my mind exist anew,
Let me taste sweet life in You.

How the pelican reveals
Christ who spills His blood and heals;
Just one drop of it has freed
All the world of sin and greed.

Jesus, You are veiled from me;
Yet I long and thirst to see
Your whole glory face to face
And to take my blessed place.
Amen.[11]

"Coeur de Jésus Hymn"

Coeur de Jésus sauvez le monde,
Que l'univers vous soit soumis,
En Vous seul notre espoir se fonde,
Seigneur, Seigneur, Vous nous l'avez promis

Vous l'avez dit, votre promesse.
Fait notre espoir, notre bonheur.
Je benirait dans ma tendresse,
Les enfants de Mon Sacré Coeur.

Coeur de Jésus sauvez le monde,
Que l'univers vous soit soumis,
En Vous seul notre espoir se fonde,
Seigneur, Seigneur, Vous nous l'avez promis

Vous l'avez dit, Sauveur fidèle,
Votre amour nous l'a révélé.
Le coeur brulant pour Moi de zele
Par le mien sera consolé.

Coeur de Jésus sauvez le monde,
Que l'univers vous soit soumis,
En Vous seul notre espoir se fonde,
Seigneur, Seigneur, Vous nous l'avez promis.

Way of the Cross

Verse. We adore you, Christ, and we bless you.
Response. Because by your holy cross you have
redeemed the world.

1. Jesus is condemned to death.
2. Jesus takes up the cross.
3. Jesus falls for the first time.
4. Jesus meets his sorrowful mother.
5. Simon of Cyrene helps Jesus carry the cross.
6. Veronica wipes the face of Jesus.
7. Jesus falls for the second time.
8. Jesus meets the women of Jerusalem.
9. Jesus falls for the third time.
10. Jesus is stripped of his garments.
11. Jesus is nailed to the cross.
12. Jesus dies on the cross.
13. Jesus is taken down from the cross.
14. Jesus is laid in the tomb.
15. Jesus is risen.

NOTES

1. This custom is known as "exposition of the Blessed Sacrament."
2. Ronald Knox, *The Window in the Wall: Reflections on the Holy Eucharist* (New York: Sheed & Ward, 1956), 2–3.

3. In Evelyn Waugh's novel about an aristocratic English Catholic family, *Brideshead Revisited*, there is a tender scene in which the young Lord Sebastian Flyte, aged nineteen, brings his new friend, Charles Ryder, home from Oxford to meet his childhood caretaker, Nanny Hawkins. Nanny Hawkins is a retired servant, living in an upstairs room of the magnificent Brideshead house. Charles Ryder, who loves architecture, describes every detail of the room, including an "oleograph of the Sacred Heart" hanging on the wall. Nanny Hawkins is a person of prayer, often found napping with her rosary in her lap, and Sebastian is very fond of her.

4. *Liturgical Novena in Honor of the Sacred Heart of Jesus*, Leaflet No. 252, copyright 1953, Apostleship of Prayer, with Ecclesiastical Approval.

5. Pierre Teilhard de Chardin, *The Divine Milieu: An Essay on the Interior Life* (New York: Harper and Row, 1960), 31.

6. The full French text is given at the close of this section.

7. Henri J. M. Nouwen, *Behold the Beauty of the Lord: Praying with Icons* (Notre Dame, Ind.: Ave Maria Press, 1987).

8. *The Heart of Spain: A Rare Exhibit of Spain's Religious Art, Antiquities and Icons* (Alexandria,

La.: Alexandria Museum of Art, 2003). See especially p. 96, "The Coronation of the Virgin."

9. Customs vary. Some churches and retreat houses have fourteen stations. Others have fifteen. In this devotion the sufferings of Jesus are always linked in our hearts to his victory over sin and death, no matter how many stations are represented or prayed.

10. Emilie Griffin, "Stations of the Cross, Inisfada" is not previously published. It was written in 1979.

11. English translation by Emilie Griffin.

Praying in the Holy Spirit

OPENING UP TO THE SPIRIT

The Holy Spirit is essential to Christian prayer. "Likewise the Spirit helps us in our weakness; for we do not know how to pray as we ought, but that very Spirit intercedes with sighs too deep for words." (Rom. 8:26) This Spirit has a number of titles: Comforter, Helper, Paraclete. Many biblical images shape our way of praying in and with the Holy Spirit. In Scripture, the Spirit of God comes down as a dove. After baptizing Jesus, John the Baptist said: "I saw the Spirit descending from heaven like a dove, and it remained on him." John continued: "I myself did not know him, but the one who sent me to baptize with water said to me, 'He on whom you see the Spirit descend and remain is the one who baptizes with the Holy Spirit.'" (John 1:32–33) Jesus, when leaving his disciples, asked them to wait in Jerusalem for the promise of the Father. "'This,' he said, 'is what you have heard from me; for John baptized with water, but you will be baptized with the Holy Spirit not many days from now.'" (Acts 1:5)

At Pentecost, the descent of the Holy Spirit was like a strong driving wind; the Spirit filled the whole house where the disciples are staying. "Divided tongues, as of fire, appeared among them, and a tongue rested on each of them." (Acts 2:3) The gathered disciples were "filled with the Holy Spirit and began to speak in other languages, as the Spirit gave them ability." (Acts 2:4) Peter interprets this outpouring as a fulfillment of Joel's prophecy:

> It will come to pass in the last days,
> God says,
> That I will pour out a portion of my spirit
> upon all flesh.
> Your sons and your daughters shall prophesy,
> Your young men shall see visions,
> Your old men shall dream dreams.
> (Acts 2:17, Catholic Study Bible)

Especially in the Acts of the Apostles, we read of many charismatic experiences: healings, raisings from the dead, prison doors opened through divine intervention.

Many of us are deeply attracted by this spiritual legacy and by contemporary manifestations of the

Spirit. But others hold back, feeling shy and wary. No doubt our temperaments affect the way we want to pray. But reticence and shyness should not keep us from being open to the Holy Spirit in prayer—and in all aspects of our lives.

Some find it easier to focus on God the Father or God the Son, addressing prayers to one or both of these divine Persons. But Catholic theology and experience tell us that all three Persons of the Blessed Trinity are One God. These three Persons of the one God are joined in a deep, mysterious, and inexhaustible love.

Some may find the Holy Spirit eludes their visual imagination. But prayer is not only visual. At a deeper level prayer involves willingness, openness, a listening attitude. We may simply need to become available to the Spirit, to open up to the Spirit's power to strengthen and enlighten us. Bit by bit we will come to accept some of the Holy Spirit's special vocabulary, words like "indwelling." The ancient Latin hymns "Veni, Creator Spiritus" and "Veni, Sancte Spiritus" can inspire us. "Inspire" is certainly the right verb for the Spirit's action in our lives.

> Come, Holy Spirit
> Enkindle in us the fire of your Love.

The Feasts of Pentecost and Holy Trinity are great openings for Spirit-filled prayer and devotion. But prayer in, with, and through the Holy Spirit can't be confined to any set time of year.

I first understood the encouragement of the Holy Spirit from a small book by Andre Louf called *Teach Us to Pray: Learning a Little about Prayer*. Louf is a cloistered Cistercian monk, an abbot, who has spent his life praying and teaching about prayer. He is also an expert on the Desert Fathers and Mothers.

When I began to be serious in prayer this book was my guide. Soon I found this astonishing statement. "For our heart is already in a *state of prayer*."

There I was, eager to pray, wanting to advance in the spiritual life, but feeling inadequate and clumsy, when the abbot spoke these words to my praying heart.

"Our heart," he says, "is already in a state of prayer. We received prayer along with grace, in our baptism. The state of grace, as we call it, at the level of the heart, actually signifies a *state of prayer*. From then on, in the profoundest depths of the self, we have a continuing contact with God. God's Holy Spirit has taken us over, has assumed complete possession of us; he has become breath of our breath and spirit of our spirit."[1]

I was even more transfixed by the next thing I read:

"He takes our heart in tow and turns it toward God." For the first time I sensed the Holy Spirit as a divine Person. I felt that Louf knew who the Spirit was, and could explain how the Spirit would help me in prayer.

"He is the spirit," Paul says, "who speaks without ceasing to our spirit and testifies to the fact that we are children of God. All the time, in fact, the spirit is calling within us and he prays, Abba-Father, with supplications and signs that cannot be put into words but never for an instant cease within our hearts." (Louf here is drawing on Rom. 8:15 and Gal. 4:6)

Listen to this wise man and take courage from his depth of soul. He knows your heart is already at prayer. "This state of prayer," he says, "is something we carry about, like a hidden treasure of which we are not consciously aware, or hardly so. Somewhere our heart is going full tilt, but we do not feel it. We are deaf to our praying heart. Love's savor escapes us. We fail to see the light in which we live."

So (as Louf showed me) it is not hard to pray when the Holy Spirit empowers us. Christian prayer is not always "charismatic" in the sense of being overt, outward, manifested in movement and song. But Christian prayer is always charismatic because the Spirit undergirds and strengthens all our prayer. That is encouraging.

CHARISMATIC PRAYER

A vivid passage in the Acts of the Apostles shows us what charismatic prayer is like. After the tremendous outpouring of the Spirit at Pentecost, the disciples began to speak in other languages. "All were amazed and perplexed, saying to one another, 'What does this mean?'" Not everyone was favorably impressed. "But others sneered and said, 'They are filled with new wine.'" (Acts 2:12–13)

How plain-spoken the Bible is sometimes. These people were so intoxicated with the Spirit that they seemed out of control. Peter defended them against this charge: "Indeed, these are not drunk, as you suppose, for it is only nine o'clock in the morning." (Acts 2:15)

Today, this same infusion of joy is sometimes seen in charismatic prayer-gatherings. Even when prayer is very formal and disciplined the life of the Spirit bubbles up.

Recently I led a retreat at Pecos Abbey in New Mexico, where a charismatic community of Benedictines—priests, brothers, and sisters—pray many times a day. They celebrate Eucharist, they offer morning and evening prayer, they conduct healing services where the Sacrament of Anointing is offered. These modern Benedictines can be heard to pray spontaneously in tongues. To the rest of the congregation their prayer sounds angelic. Some heavenly door (it seems) has been opened and God's amazing grace is showered on everyone.

HEALING PRAYER

Christians ought to practice healing prayer without doubt or hesitation. There is plenty of precedent for it in the life of Jesus, in the lives of the early disciples as well. Contemporary people sometimes think such signs and wonders ended in the first century. But major outcroppings of spiritual healing have occurred since New Testament times. And Jesus did not suggest any time frame: "These signs will accompany those who believe: by using my name they will cast out demons; they will speak in new tongues; they will pick up snakes in their hands, and if they drink any deadly thing it will not hurt them; they will lay their hands on the sick and they will recover." (Mk. 16:17)

One of the greatest encouragements to healing prayer in the Holy Spirit is to read attentively the Acts of the Apostles. This book, a densely packed account of the earliest days of Christianity, details many surprising events. One heartwarming passage tells of Paul's work in Corinth: "God did extraordinary miracles through Paul, so that when handkerchiefs or aprons that had touched his skin were brought to the sick, their diseases left them, and the evil spirits came out of them." (Acts 19:11–12) There's even a touch of humor in this passage. When some traveling exorcists try to duplicate Paul's spiritual feats, saying, "I adjure you by the Jesus whom Paul proclaims," the evil spirit replies, "Jesus I know, and Paul I know, but who are you?"

Sometimes we moderns are intimidated by the wondrous character of these stories. We suppose that some exaggerations must have been at work. Hasn't some of this been embellished by primitive belief? Were these demonic possessions really as noted, or were they mental illnesses? How can we translate these events into their contemporary equivalents? For the purpose of prayer we can set these concerns aside. The Acts of the Apostles tells us that the Holy Spirit is powerful, active, and available to us in prayer. Our faith needs to be empowered and strengthened. Where healing is concerned, we need the faith and the courage to ask.

Prayer for healing should not be arrogant, peremptory, or demanding. Every prayer-request is offered with the sentiment: "God's will be done."

GIFTS OF THE SPIRIT

Paul writes to the Galatians about the fruit of the Spirit: love, joy, peace, patience, kindness, generosity, faithfulness, gentleness, and self-control. (Gal. 5:22) "There is," he adds, "no law against such things." Paul describes these gifts in sharp contrast to the desires of the flesh: fornication, impurity, licentiousness, idolatry, sorcery, enmities, strife, jealousy, anger, quarrels, dissensions, factions, envy, drunkenness, carousing, and "things like these." His list covers the topic fairly well. "If we live by the Spirit, let us also be guided by the Spirit. Let us not become conceited, competing against one another, envying one another." (Gal. 5:25–26)

Paul is writing about spiritual formation and transformation. The fruit of the Spirit, the guidance of the

Spirit, reshapes our desires when we consent to be guided by the Spirit. Prayer is one way to open ourselves to this kind of transformation.

When I was getting started in the spiritual life, I wrote down the list of "fruits of the Spirit." I counted nine of them. Then I added another list, found in Isaiah 11, in which the spirit of the Lord is described that rests upon the coming Messiah:

the spirit of wisdom and understanding
the spirit of counsel and might
the spirit of knowledge and the fear of the Lord.
(Isa. 11:2)

These, too, I added to my list, and kept them with me as encouragements to the life of the Spirit. My husband jokingly called them my "Baskin Robbins flavors."

I loved the joke. But I knew only too well I couldn't order these blessings by the scoop. These would be entirely at God's discretion, lavished on me not because I deserved them, but because of the generosity of God.

It's an interesting situation. If we cooperate with God's grace, we will receive the fruit of the Spirit. If we don't, we'll take a chance with our lives, present and future. But we can't earn the grace. God dispenses it, not according to our merits, but the infinite merits of Christ.

SAMPLE TEXTS

"Veni, Creator Spiritus"

Veni, Creator Spiritus
Mentes tuorum visita
Imple superna gratia
Quae tu creasti pectora.

Qui diceris Paraclitus
Altissimi donum Dei,
Fons vivus, ignis, caritas,
Et spiritualis unctio.

Tu septiformis munere,
Digitus paternae dexterae,
Tu rite promissum Patris,
Sermone ditans guttura,

Accende lumen sensibus,
Infunde amorem cordibus,
Infirma nostri corporis
Virtute firmans perpeti.

Hostem repellas longius,
Pacemque dones protinus:
Ductore sic te praevio
Vitemus omne noxium.

Per te sciamus da Patrem,
Noscamus atque Filium,
Teque utriusque Spiritum
Credamus omni tempore.

Deo Patri sit gloria,
Et Filio, qui a mortuis
Surrexit, ac Paraclito,
In saeculorum saecula. Amen.

"Come, Creator Spirit"
(Translation of "Veni, Creator Spiritus")

Come, Creator Spirit
Fill our space
Flood our hearts and minds
with your sovereign grace.

Paraclete, you give
Gifts of God's appointing
Living fountain, loving flame
Spiritual anointing.

You the Sevenfold Gift,
God's hand, God's token,
You are the Father's promise
Shouted, spoken.

Strike our hearts ablaze
Drench us with your love
Strengthen us with power
From above.

Drive the Enemy away.
Peace be here!
Lead us far from evil
And from fear.

Let us know the Father
May we see the Son
In your Spirit
Ever One.

Glory to the Father
And the Son from death ascending
In your Spirit
World without ending. Amen.[2]

"Veni, Sancte Spiritus"

Veni, Sancte Spiritus
Et emitte caelitus
Lucis tuae radium.
Veni, pater pauperum,
Veni, dator munerum,
Veni, lumen cordium.

Consolator optime,
Dulcis hospes animae,
Dulce refrigerium;
in labore requies,
in aestu temperies,
in fletu solarium.

O lux beatissima,
Reple cordis intima
tuorum fidelium!
Sine tuo nomine
Nihil est in homine
Nihil est innoxium.

Lava quod est sordidum,
Riga quod est aridum,
Sana quod est saucium;
Flecte quod est rigidum,
Fove quod est frigidum,
Rege quod est devium.

Da tuis fidelibus
in te confidentibus
sacrum septenarium;
Da virtutis meritum,
Da salutis exitum,
Da perenne gaudium. Amen.

"Come, Holy Spirit"
(Translation of "Veni, Sancte Spiritus")

Come, Holy Spirit
Shine your blesséd light
Beam on us
From your lovely height.

Father of the poor
Warm us with your gaze
With your treasures that endure
Hearts will blaze.

Be our consolation
Our soul's guest
Be our transformation;
Be our rest.

Refuge from our struggles
Respite from our heat
In a time of sorrow
You are sweet.

Holy Radiance
Fill our empty spaces
Till we overflow
With your sovereign graces.

For without your Name
No one is secure;
Everything is shame.
Nothing can endure.

Wash our sins away
For our souls are dry
Flood our hearts today
From on high.

Rule our stubborn will
When we go astray
Melt our icy souls
With your ray.

Give to faithful ones,
Those who have been true
Sevenfold sacred Gifts
To make us new.

Spirit, may we spend
Endless life above.
Be our sweetness, be our friend,
Be our love.[3]

NOTES

1. Andre Louf, *Teach Us to Pray: Learning a Little about God* (New York: Paulist Press, 1974), 18–19.
2. Translation of "Veni, Creator Spiritus," by Emilie Griffin, 2005.
3. Translation of "Veni, Sancte Spiritus," by Emilie Griffin, 2005.

5

The Blessed Virgin Mary

WHAT MARIAN PRAYER IS ALL ABOUT

Catholics honor Mary the Mother of Jesus in many ways. Most Catholics feel close to Mary the Mother of the Lord. There is an intimate bond between their love of Jesus and their love of his mother. Mary is often called "our mother" and she has a very long list of exalted titles and rich devotions in her honor. The earliest Catholic settlers in North America put America under Mary's protection; today American Catholics still believe that Mary is their guardian.

Devotion to Mary is rooted in the Incarnation. Christians view Jesus as the Word made Flesh. Because Christianity is incarnational, teaching that God became man and continues to be both God and man, Jesus' mother has a role in our redemption. She is an integral part of the salvation story.

Several of the most important Marian prayers are scriptural. The first of these is the Hail Mary (*Ave Maria* in Latin), which begins with the words of the Archangel Gabriel to Mary at the Annunciation. Gabriel's words to Mary are sometimes called his salutation, or greeting:

> Hail Mary, full of grace
> The Lord is with thee.
> Blessed art thou among women.

The prayer continues with words that are very ancient, their origin lost in the earliest history of Christianity:

> and blessed is the fruit of your womb, Jesus.
> Holy Mary, Mother of God,
> pray for us sinners
> now and at the hour of our death. Amen.

The second Marian prayer found in Scripture is the Canticle of Mary, also known by its Latin name, *The Magnificat*.

> My soul proclaims the greatness of the Lord;
> my spirit rejoices in God my savior.
> For he has looked upon his handmaid's lowliness;

behold, from now on all ages will call me blessed.
The Mighty One has done great things for me,
and holy is his name.

His mercy is from age to age
to those who fear him.
He has shown might with his arm,
dispersed the arrogant of mind and heart.
He has thrown down the rulers from their thrones
but lifted up the lowly.
The hungry he has filled with good things;
the rich he has sent away empty.
He has helped Israel his servant,
remembering his mercy,
according to his promise to our fathers,
to Abraham and to his descendants forever.
(Lk. 1:46–55)

The Canticle of Mary is a rich opportunity for
prayer. In praying it we stand with Mary and look at
the Lord from her point of view. It is a prayer of praise
and gratitude: "the Mighty One has done great things
for me." In a sense, Mary's Canticle is a lesson in how
to pray. In it she expresses tremendous confidence in
the power of God and his compassion and justice to
his people. "His mercy is from age to age to those
who fear him." Almost any phrase in this beautiful
prayer can become a deep and rich meditation. The
prayer also highlights one of Mary's virtues that we
long to imitate: her simplicity. She describes herself as

a lowly handmaid. Here we notice that Mary's attitude
in prayer is grateful, humble, uncomplicated. By praying her Canticle we hope to assume her attitude as
well.

THE NATIVITY SCENE

Christmas—the Feast of the Nativity—is one of our
principal devotions to Mary in her role as mother. Not
just Catholics but many other Christians have adopted
this form of devotion today. At Christmas time, the
crèche (a French word for cradle scene) is found in
many homes and churches. Jesus, the Christ-child, is
at the center of this scene, with Mary his mother and
Joseph his father adoring him. At a distance, the shepherds, wise men, and angels—together with domestic
animals of various kinds—also revere the Holy Family.
Latin Americans have a Christmas devotion called
Posadas—the inns. In it they reenact the story of Mary
and Joseph going from inn to inn, looking for a place
to stay so that Mary can bear the child.

The Nativity scene reminds us that the power of
Christian devotion is embedded in, and flows from, a
story. In fact, the whole of Judaeo-Christian religion
is revealed in the form of story, enfleshed. God's presence is with us in the middle of ordinary life.

So, merely visiting the crèche in a church, or
spending a few prayerful minutes with your crèche at
home, is a chance for devotion: to adore Jesus as the
Holy Child ("holy infant, so tender and mild") and to

be drawn in by the vivid incarnational nature of Christian faith. The Nativity reminds us clearly of Mary's role. From her loving concern for the Christ-child we appreciate her compassion for all of us.

Christmas plays are another form of genuinely Catholic devotion. I was first introduced to the Christmas play in my high school days, and surprised by the power of a pageant in which clumsy high schoolers portrayed the shepherds, the wise men, the angels, the Holy Family. In spite of their awkwardness there was a hush, an awe in the moment.

If you attend a Christmas play, however awkward or rough the acting style, consider it an opportunity for devotion and prayer.

THE ANGELUS

The Angelus is an ancient prayer addressed in part to Mary, which recaptures the Annunciation scene. It probably began in the Middle Ages; we have our best clue to its origins in the fourteenth century when Pope John XXII began to encourage the saying of this prayer by attaching the special encouragement of indulgences to it. The words of the prayer re-create the scriptural scene of Gabriel's announcement to Mary.

Verse: The Angel of the Lord declared unto Mary.
Response: And she conceived of the Holy Spirit.
    Hail Mary, full of grace, the Lord is with thee . . .

Verse: Behold the handmaid of the Lord.
Response: Be it done to me according to your word.
  Hail Mary, full of grace, the Lord is with thee . . .
Verse: And the Word was made flesh,
Response: And dwelt among us.
  Hail Mary, full of grace, the Lord is with thee . . .
Verse: Pray for us, O Holy Mother of God,
Response: That we may be made worthy of the
  promises of Christ.

Let us pray:
Pour forth, we beseech you, O Lord, your grace into
our hearts; that, as we have known the incarnation of
Christ, your son, by the message of an angel, so by his
passion and cross we may be brought to the glory of his
resurrection. Through the same Christ, our Lord. Amen.

The Angelus addresses Mary with deep reverence
and devotion but also locates her within the larger
story of salvation. As the prayer closes, it is clear that
our petitions are to God, with Mary interceding. This
is good Catholic prayer.

Recently I was glad to see this prayer invoked by
the American scholar and journalist Peter Steinfels at
the end of his book, *A People Adrift: The Crisis Facing
the American Catholic Church*. Steinfels had outlined
a number of sources of difficulty and dissension over
the last several decades of American Catholicism.
While the tone of his book was respectful, it was not
a work of devotion. Yet when he came to summarize
and look to the future, he turned to Mary as interces-

sor, especially invoking the Angelus prayer. Steinfels was completing his book on March 25, 2003, the Feast of the Annunciation, which turned his thoughts to Mary. However, the date was not what struck me, so much as the appropriateness of his placing the difficulties of the Church in Mary's lap. As she cared for the Christ-child, Catholics hope Mary will help care for the Church in time of need. This caring aspect of Mary evokes the words of a Christmas carol:

> What child is this who laid to rest
> in Mary's lap is sleeping?

FAMILIAR PRAYERS TO MARY

Most Catholics know by heart several prayers addressed to Mary. One of these, of course, is the Hail Mary. Other prayers to Mary are commonly recited. One is the *Memorare*, a Latin word (and the first word of the prayer) which means "remember":

> Remember, O most gracious Virgin Mary
> That never was it known
> That anyone who fled to your protection,
> Desired your help, or sought your intercession
> Was left unaided.
> Inspired by this confidence,
> We fly unto you,
> O Virgin of virgins, our mother.
> To you we come, before you we kneel,
> Sinful and sorrowful.

O Mother of the Word Incarnate
Despise not our petitions
But in your mercy hear and answer us. Amen.

Heavenly Queen

One of the ways that Mary is addressed in prayer is as the Queen of Heaven, first among the saints. One familiar Catholic prayer addressing her as Queen is known in Latin as the *Salve Regina*.

Hail, holy queen,
Mother of mercy,
our life, our sweetness and our hope.
To thee do we cry,
poor banished children of Eve.
To thee do we send up our sighs,
mourning and weeping in this valley of tears.
Turn then, most gracious advocate,
thine eyes of mercy toward us,
and after this our exile
show us the blessed fruit of thy womb,
Jesus.
O clement, o loving, o sweet virgin Mary,
Pray for us, o holy mother of God,
that we may be made worthy of the promises of
Christ. Amen.

This prayer presents us with a picture of Mary in her role as our advocate with God. Also it is a prayer of repentance, in which we admit our inadequacy and ask Mary to help us along the path of life.

Mary is considered first among the saints. When we pray to her, it is because we see her as highly favored by God the Father, and powerful and influential with Jesus, who is God the Son. Often, Catholics address prayers to Mary simply because they love her and feel close to her.

Once, in order to express my own devotion to Mary, I wrote a brief poem:

> How shall I
> That virgin hardly ever was, in thought,
> and now in fact can never be
> How shall I
> with you unite
> Beloved Mother of the world?
>
> Oh, woman filled with grace
> and overflowing,
> teach me to be
> all that you are
> just so far as this little self
> can grow
> to your great sanctity.

The Rosary

One of the best-known prayers addressed to Mary is the Rosary, so called because Mary's flower is the

Rose. A set of beads is used, usually five sequences of ten beads, making a circlet of some fifty beads, together with three beads for the introductory prayers, and a small crucifix which serves as the beginning point of saying the prayers. One begins by holding the crucifix and reciting, devoutly, the Apostle's Creed. Then three small beads follow. One holds the bead and recites a prayer "on" the bead, then moves to the next. Then follow the ten-bead sets, or "decades" of the Rosary.

Rosary prayers are organized according to a scheme, in which the Hail Mary, the Our Father, and the prayer usually known as the Glory Be are combined in alternation. But the Rosary is also a set of meditations on the life of Christ and the life of Mary, meditations that are made in combination with the repeated saying of the prayers. The customs and practices of this structured prayer began centuries ago when most Christians could not read. Thus, the prayer became a way of keeping unlettered people connected with the great mysteries of Christian faith. The Joyful Mysteries include the Annunciation, the Visitation, the Nativity, the Presentation, and the Finding of the Child Jesus in the Temple. The Sorrowful Mysteries are the Agony in the Garden, the Scourging, the Crowning with Thorns, the Carrying of the Cross, and the Death of Jesus. The Glorious Mysteries are the Resurrection, the Ascension, the Descent of the Holy Spirit upon the Apostles, the Assumption, and the Crowning of Mary as Queen of Heaven. For some centuries these fifteen mysteries dominated the practice of saying the Rosary. Recently, however, the Luminous Mysteries were added by Pope John Paul II. They are the Baptism of Jesus, the Wedding Feast at Cana, the Proclamation of the Kingdom of God, the Transfiguration, and the Institution of the Eucharist. All these mysteries are customarily assigned to be prayed on certain days of the week.

For some people, the Rosary is the principal prayer of their lives, one which keeps them in touch with both Jesus and Mary and with the central mysteries of faith. Since the Rosary begins with the recitation of the Apostle's Creed, it is also an affirmation of faith that comes as part of daily devotions. Others use the Rosary especially in times of trouble, danger, or loss. Many American Catholics turned to the Rosary after the tragedies of September 11, 2001.

It takes some skill and practice, I find, to say the Rosary using both the repeated prayers and meditating on the mysteries at the same time. But once that skill takes hold, the Rosary opens up a rich world of devotion.

John Paul II asked us to consider the Rosary as a form of contemplation, and Mary as our model for contemplation. In praying the Rosary we may assume the vantage point of Mary. "Therefore Mary's gaze," the Holy Father wrote, "ever filled with adoration and wonder, would never leave him (her Son)." At times, he said, her look would be questioning, sometimes penetrating, often a look of sorrow, a gaze radiant with the joy of the Resurrection, or else, on the day of Pentecost, a gaze afire with the outpouring of the Spirit. To follow this guidance, using the Rosary in contemplative style, is an exercise of the religious imagination.

Sally Cunneen, in commenting on the Rosary, points out the especial comfort of touching and holding the beads. This devotion is by its very nature incarnational.[1]

To capture the experience of praying the Rosary, I once wrote the following:

Glorious Mysteries

Along these beads
round wood slipping through fingers
my prayers whisper
and for a time
I stand where Mary stood:
seeing Him raised
seeing Him ascend
hearing the Spirit blow
into the upper room.
Then, she too is raised to bliss,
with Heaven's host.
With her, our hopes are lifted up,
our sorrows plucked away.
Glory.
Just a glimpse of it,
told in whispers
five times ten
along a string of wooden beads.

LITANY OF THE BLESSED VIRGIN

Litanies are an ancient form of Catholic prayer. There are a number of these, expressing different aspects of Christian devotion. The Litany of the Blessed Virgin can be used privately or in a group, as a way of honoring Mary the Mother of God. Notice that the prayer is first addressed to the three Persons of the Trinity, and only then turns its attention to the Blessed Mother.

Lord, have mercy on us.
Christ, have mercy on us.
Lord, have mercy on us.
Christ, hear us.
Christ, graciously hear us.
God the Father of Heaven, have mercy on us.
God the Son, Redeemer of the world,
have mercy on us.
God the Holy Spirit, have mercy on us.
Holy Trinity, one God, have mercy on us.
Holy Mary, pray for us.
Holy Mother of God, pray for us.
Mother of Christ, pray for us.
Mother most pure, pray for us.
Mother most chaste, pray for us.
Mother inviolate, pray for us.
Mother undefiled, pray for us.
Mother most amiable, pray for us.
Mother most admirable, pray for us.

Mother of good counsel, pray for us.
Mother of our Creator, pray for us.
Mother of our Savior, pray for us.
Virgin most prudent, pray for us.
Virgin most venerable, pray for us.
Virgin most renowned, pray for us.
Virgin most powerful, pray for us.
Virgin most merciful, pray for us.
Virgin most faithful, pray for us.
Mirror of justice, pray for us.
Seat of wisdom, pray for us.
Cause of our joy, pray for us.
Spiritual vessel, pray for us.
Vessel of honor, pray for us.
Vessel of singular devotion, pray for us.
Mystical rose, pray for us.
Tower of David, pray for us.
Tower of ivory, pray for us.
House of gold, pray for us.
Ark of the covenant, pray for us.
Gate of heaven, pray for us.
Morning star, pray for us.
Health of the sick, pray for us.
Refuge of sinners, pray for us.
Comforter of the afflicted, pray for us.
Help of Christians, pray for us.
Queen of angels, pray for us.
Queen of Patriarchs, pray for us.

Queen of Prophets, pray for us.
Queen of Apostles, pray for us.
Queen of Martyrs, pray for us.
Queen of Confessors, pray for us.
Queen of Virgins, pray for us.
Queen conceived without original sin, pray for us.
Queen assumed into heaven, pray for us.
Queen of the most holy rosary, pray for us.
Queen of peace, pray for us.

Lamb of God, who takes away the sins of the
    world,
spare us, O Lord.
Lamb of God, who takes away the sins of the
    world,
graciously hear us, Lord.
Verse: Pray for us, O Holy Mother of God.
Response: That we may be made worthy of the
promises of Christ.
(*Note that the closing prayer addresses the Lord God
first, then asks for Mary's intercession.*)
Let us pray.
Grant, we beseech you, O Lord God, that we, your
servants, may enjoy perpetual health of soul and
body; and by the glorious intercession of blessed
Mary, ever virgin, may be delivered from present
sorrows and rejoice in eternal happiness. Through
Christ, our Lord. Amen.

SAMPLE TEXTS FOR MARIAN PRAYER[2]

The Hail Mary (*Ave Maria*)

Hail Mary, full of grace
The Lord is with thee.
Blessed art thou among women.
and blessed is the fruit of thy womb, Jesus.

Holy Mary, Mother of God,
pray for us sinners
now and at the hour of our death. Amen.

Hail, Holy Queen (*Salve Regina*)

Hail, holy queen,
Mother of mercy,
our life, our sweetness and our hope.
To thee do we cry,
poor banished children of Eve.
To thee do we send up our sighs,
mourning and weeping in this valley of tears.
Turn then, most gracious advocate,
thine eyes of mercy toward us,
and after this our exile
show us the blessed fruit of thy womb, Jesus.
O clement, o loving, o sweet virgin Mary,
Pray for us, o holy mother of God,
that we may be made worthy of the promises of
Christ. Amen.

The Lord's Prayer, also called the Our Father

Our Father, who art in heaven,
Hallowed be thy name;
Thy kingdom come; thy will be done;
On earth as it is in heaven.
Give us this day our daily bread;
And forgive us our trespasses
As we forgive those who trespass against us.
And lead us not into temptation
But deliver us from evil. Amen.

Glory Be

Glory be to the Father
and to the Son
and to the Holy Spirit.
As it was in the beginning
is now
and ever shall be.
World without end, Amen.

NOTE

1. See Sally Cunneen, "The Rosary," in *Awake My Soul: Contemporary Catholics on Traditional Devotions*, ed. James Martin (Chicago: Loyola Press, 2004), 63–68.
2. The Our Father, Hail Mary, and Glory Be are used in combination in the recitation of the Rosary.

6

Praying to Angels and Saints

HEAVENLY INTERCESSORS

When you visit any major museum or notable historic church, you may be struck by the importance of saints and angels in the history of Christian spirituality. At the Cloisters Museum in New York City, one passes through an entire room of statues of Our Lady, holding the Child Jesus in her arms. Representing different European ethnic groups, they form a composite and vivid picture of both Mother and Child. Such visual power and storytelling impact can quicken our devotion. Yet we moderns sometimes wonder if we can develop the same relationship to angels and saints that our ancestors had. Have we lost our enthusiasm for saints and angels, at least where devotion is concerned?

Growing up as a Protestant child in New Orleans I was alternately envious of Catholic devotion to the saints and scandalized by it. Why couldn't Catholics pray directly to God? I wondered. Later, as an adult, and a convert to Catholic faith, I learned the answer. Catholics can pray directly to God, and they often do.

But Catholic devotion has long relied on the intercession of the saints and the angels in heaven, who are thought to have a more direct knowledge of God than we have here and now. Angels may be asked to carry our prayers to the throne of God and gain God's attention there. In a similar fashion, saints are thought to be powerful intercessors, sometimes specializing in particular issues that affect our lives, everything from healing to marriage to finding lost articles. If you are attentive at Mass you will notice that prayers are offered to God by us together with the angels and saints, the whole company of heaven.

For a long time I honored this practice, but I did not fully grasp it myself. Then, during the 1980s I began a long research study on the life of a holy Catholic woman, Cornelia Connelly, the founder of the Sisters of the Holy Child Jesus. I was intending to write a book about her, concentrating on her years in Louisiana during the 1830s. At the time of my research, Cornelia had been declared Servant of God Cornelia Connelly: the first step in canonization. More recently, she has been declared Venerable Cornelia Connelly.

Catholics are not allowed to build shrines for departed holy people until they have been officially canonized. But, to my surprise, I learned that an Episcopalian couple in Natchez had built a shrine to Cornelia. I visited their home in Natchez and other places where she had lived—in Philadelphia; Grand Coteau, Louisiana; and in the south of England— making, in effect, a Cornelia Connelly pilgrimage. In this way I came to understand the roots of Catholic devotion to saints.

As part of my study I came to know many stories about Cornelia Connelly, and I could quote many of her sayings and prayers by heart.

> Trim thy vine,
> Cut it to the quick,
> But in thy great mercy root it not yet up.[1]

When I was working in the Connelly archives in Pennsylvania, I read many of Cornelia's letters and came to know her handwriting, her particular forms of expression. One day a box was opened by the archivist containing things that had belonged to Cornelia. I was deeply touched.

I found myself thinking: so this is how devotion to the saints began. Others in her religious community remarked that I had a strong devotion to (using their language) Blessed Mother Foundress. I began to enjoy this connection with Cornelia, her life, her style of prayer. I was affected by her life-story. Even more, I was moved by her way of giving everything to God.

For me, devotion to the saints has mostly come about through study of their lives. Others may be moved by paintings and statues. Instead, I have been moved by the life-stories and writings of the saints.

One way Catholics begin to identify with saints is by choosing a saint's name for the sacrament of confirmation. What a weighty decision that can be! In my case it was easy enough, since I was born on July 22, the feast of St. Mary Magdalene. By virtue of my birth date, Mary Magdalene became my patron.

But what a tender example she gave me! She led me to the other Marys as well, Mary of Bethany and Mary the Mother of the Lord. Perhaps I was attracted by what I thought was Mary Magdalene's worldliness, the high drama of her life-story. Now I know that much of what I believed about her at first was probably fanciful. But Scripture tells us how closely she followed Jesus; that he had driven seven devils out of her; and she was the first to see him after his Resurrection. My way of devotion was to *identify* with St. Mary Magdalene.

I have been attracted to other saints mostly through their writings: St. Teresa of Avila, St. John of the Cross, St. Ignatius Loyola, St. Therese of Lisieux. I have read their life-stories, their own works on prayer. I have sometimes used the prayers attributed to them.

When I reflect on the saints who have inspired me, I would mention St. Paul first—and foremost. Women are supposed to identify with women saints, but Paul has long been my favorite. His adventures, his daring, his mystical depth, his forthrightness, his tender love of Timothy and other disciples, all these have deeply formed me in faith.

From this level of devotion it is only a short step to intercessory prayer. We address the saints in heaven because we know they are alive, perhaps more alive than we are. We tell them our concerns. We ask them to pray for us.

GUARDIAN ANGELS

Many Catholics are taught devotion to the angels when they learn their childhood prayers:

> Angel of God, my guardian dear,
> To whom his love commits me here,
> Ever this night be at my side,
> To light and guard,
> To rule and guide. Amen.

My own devotion to the angels began rather differently—through literature. In my first reading of John Milton's *Paradise Lost*, when I was about nineteen, I discovered archangels. Nothing in Scripture had prepared me for Milton's description of the Archangel Raphael on his way to earth to counsel Adam and Eve:

Down thither prone in flight
He speeds, and through the vast ethereal sky
Sails between worlds and worlds, with steady wings
Now on the polar winds, then with quick fan
Winnows the buxom air . . .
At once on the eastern gulf of Paradise
He lights, and to his proper shape returns
A seraph winged;

Milton goes on to describe Raphael's six wings, each
pair shading "his lineaments divine." He describes the
wings as "downy gold/and colors dipped in heaven."
The effect on me was remarkable. I felt I had actually
seen an angel.

The Roman Catholic Church has a feast day for
guardian angels on October 2. Writing about this feast
from the vantage point of a Benedictine monastery in
Minnesota, Kathleen Norris writes: "It has to do with
us, this feast. What we long for, and see, and do not
see. 'And the angels are here,' says St. Bernard, whispering like a child." Norris glimpses two crows
between herself and the brilliant autumn trees, maple
and ash. Their cries strike her as mysterious, like St.
Bernard's question to the angels. *What are we*,
Bernard asks, *that you make yourself known to us?*[2]

ST. MICHAEL ARCHANGEL

After becoming Catholic I understood for the first
time that Catholics actually were praying to angels as

they did to saints. In the days before Vatican II the
Mass ended with a prayer addressed to Michael the
Archangel:

> St. Michael the Archangel, defend us in battle. Be our
> protection against the wickedness and snares of the devil.
> May God rebuke him, we humbly pray, and do you, O
> Prince of the Heavenly Host, by the divine power thrust
> into hell Satan and the other evil spirits who roam the
> world seeking the ruin of souls. Amen.

Inside my Bible I have tucked a prayer pamphlet
offering devotions to St. Michael. Its author, Father
Lawrence G. Lovasik, S.V.D., insists that devotion to
St. Michael the Archangel is "as old as the Church and
even older, because it . . . existed in the time of the
Jewish synagogue. It is found in both the Eastern and
the Western Church."

Father Lovasik identifies St. Michael as the Patron
and Protector of the Universal Church.

Belief in angels is very ancient and common to all
three Middle Eastern religions: Judaism, Christianity,
and Islam. Today the Archangel Michael with the
other archangels is honored in a Catholic feast of the
universal church, September 29. From the beginning,
for all believers, Michael was the best-known and most
venerated archangel, the only archangel honored with
his own feast day for many centuries. In the ninth century feast days for Gabriel and Raphael were added. In
the eighth century the Roman Catholic leadership cau-
tioned that the only archangels to be addressed in

prayer by name are Michael, Gabriel, and Raphael, because they are the only ones named in the canonical Scriptures.

Even today St. Michael is honored as a protector against evil, an angel of justice who will plead in favor of souls on the final day of judgment. Michael is also known as the prince of the heavenly host.

His name, like the other names of archangels, ends with the syllable "el." "El," in Hebrew, indicates connection with God, as in such names as Bethel and Israel.

Michael is mentioned often in Scripture: in Daniel 10:13, 21, and 12:1. "At that time Michael, the great prince, the protector of your people, shall arise. There shall be a time of anguish, such as has never occurred since nations first came into existence. But at that time your people shall be delivered, everyone who is found written in the book, some to everlasting life and some to shame and everlasting contempt. Those who are wise shall shine like the brightness of the sky, and those who lead many to righteousness, like the stars forever and ever."

Michael is also identified as an archangel in Jude 9; he is mentioned in Revelation 12:7, in a famous passage in which a war breaks out in heaven and Michael overcomes Satan and throws him down from heaven to earth, and other fallen angels with him. This biblical scene is developed by the Protestant poet, John Milton, who writes, in *Paradise Lost*,

him the Almighty Power
hurled headlong flaming from the ethereal sky
with deadly ruin and combustion down
to bottomless perdition, there to dwell
in adamantine chains and penal fire.[3]

INTERPRETING ANGELS

In the history of the Western Christian Church there have been many commentators on angels, most remarkably St. Thomas Aquinas, who tells us (using a combination of scriptural revelation and philosophical reasoning) that angels are a different order of beings, pure disembodied intelligences, whose way of knowing is intuitive. Unlike us here on earth, the angels enjoy the vision of God and are completely obedient to God's will (not counting of course, the fallen angels who refused to accept God's plan).

Because there is a rich literature about angels, it is easy to dismiss them as purely literary. However, a number of modern writers, including the twentieth-century Thomist philosopher Mortimer Adler[4] and the Protestant evangelist Billy Graham, have taken angels seriously.

Of course we find angels in Scripture. Jesus mentions to the disciples that he could ask his Heavenly Father to send angels to rescue him. "Do you think that I cannot call upon my Father and he will not provide me at this moment with more than twelve legions of angels?" (Mt. 26:53) But Jesus will not abuse the privilege of calling on his Father's angelic rescuers. He explains that the Passion must take place; the intervention of the angels would interrupt the divine plan prophesied in Scripture.

Angels also appear in the vision of John, which appears in the Book of Revelation:

> I looked again and heard the voices of many
> angels who surrounded the throne and the living
> creatures and the elders. They were countless in
> number and they cried out in a loud voice:
> "Worthy is the lamb that was slain
> to receive power and riches, wisdom and strength
> honor and glory and blessing."
> (Rev. 5:11–12)

PERSONAL DEVOTION TO ANGELS

Recently, while attending the *Heart of Spain* art exhibit held in Alexandria, Louisiana, I found my devotion to the angels ignited once again.

The exhibit had been lent by the Spanish people to help celebrate the 200th anniversary of the Louisiana Purchase. The exhibit was perhaps not meant to be devotional. But for me, it was. In a spirit of prayer I went from room to room, viewing about a hundred (mostly religious) works of art by such artists as Goya, El Greco, Velasquez, Murillo, and others.

As we moved into the Great Hall—not the last room of the exhibit but the largest one, and in some ways the most climactic—were four paintings of archangels.

The Archangels Michael, Uriel, Raphael, and Seathiel—in courtly period clothes—were hanging high on the walls. They are part of a series of seven archangels painted by Bartolomé Román about 1614, at a time when devotion to the angels and archangels was enormously popular throughout Europe and the Americas.

There is no doubt that angelology—the study of angels—developed great popularity in the Middle Ages and continued through later centuries. Elaborate ways of depicting the archangels had to do with the meanings of their names and the roles they were presumed to play.

Michael, "who is like God," carries a spear and a palm; Gabriel, "fortified of God," carries a branch of white lilies and an oil lamp; Uricl, "fire of God," has a flaming sword; Seathiel, "prayer of God," holds a vessel of incense; Barachiel, "blessing of God," holds a mass of roses. In golden letters the meaning of each name is given, with exhortations to "obey divine inspirations," "reach the virtue of obedience," "persevere against temptations," "follow the will of God."

In the tradition of the Catholic Church, angels are pure spirits, intelligent beings endowed with free will, who take part in the beatific vision (the face-to-face vision with God, which is possible in heaven). They are thus enabled to help humanity and can be asked to do so.

PATRON SAINTS OF NATIONS

The Roman Catholic Church celebrates the feast days of saints throughout the Christian year. Many of these feast days are also national in character. St. Patrick is well known as the patron saint of the Irish and his feast day is kept more raucously in the United States than in Ireland itself. St. Joseph's Day is widely celebrated by the Italians. In New Orleans the Italian community celebrates his feast (March 19) with St. Joseph's Altars. These altars combine offerings of food with pictures, candles, and statuary, thanking St. Joseph for his help in dealing with a time of famine. Often one can tell the identity of national patron saints from the names of ethnic churches dedicated to them. A Hungarian church is often named for St. Stephen. St. George is the patron saint of England, and one often finds Anglican (Protestant Episcopal) churches dedicated to him.[5]

Today there has been quite a revival of interest in the Celtic saints of England, Scotland, and Ireland. Scholars have been recovering and writing their history. The Northumbria Community in England, not far from the Scottish border, has compiled a book called *Celtic Daily Prayer*, which provides brief liturgies and prayers for many of the Celtic saints: Brendan, Brigid, Aidan, and Cuthbert among them. The Northumbria Community is not Roman Catholic. They are British Christians from various traditions, holding to an ancient form of prayer, influenced by love of Christ, and practicing ancient Christian disciplines.[6]

In answer to the question, "Why Celtic?" The Northumbria authors write: "The 'old paths' around us here in Northumbria resound with the testimony of the remarkable men and women who simply loved God and followed Jesus wherever the Spirit impelled and empowered them to go." As they researched and studied their own native saints, who in turn had been inspired by the Desert Fathers and Mothers, the Northumbrians felt led to create a modern version of their ancient spiritual practice. "We found that many of the lessons they taught gave us hope and coherence on our own journey: that people matter more than things, and relationships more than reputation; that prayer and action, contemplation and involvement, all belong together."[7] At the same time they say they are resisting the temptation to hark back to a mythical golden age, which probably never existed. Still, it is clear that they are stirred by the early centuries of "these islands," perhaps by the seventh century most of all.

I stay in touch with the British saints—those honored by the Anglican Church worldwide—in another quite simple way. For my daily calendar I use an Oxford pocket diary, which a kind friend sends me from England each year. On its pages I find saints remembered. Some of these are the same as those in the Roman calendar. Others, like Evelyn Underhill, have not been formally canonized, but are honored

by the Anglicans for their lives of fidelity and devotion. Anglicans, too, consider themselves Catholics,
although they are not in communion with the
Roman See. My experience has been that both
Anglicans and Eastern Orthodox Christians are praying in the Catholic tradition: Roman Catholics have
much in common with these faith-filled sisters and
brothers.

NONVERBAL DEVOTION
TO ANGELS AND SAINTS

In Catholic bookstores—in churches, retreat houses,
and on street corners—various holy objects are offered
for sale. Some of these are small images or pictures of
saints and angels: prayer cards, medals, statues, prayer-
pamphlets. Most of the prayer cards feature both a picture of the saint and a written prayer.

But to hold such an object, and to regard it, is a
kind of devotion. This form of nonverbal prayer has
long been practiced and honored in the Catholic tradition. It is like having a picture on your desk or
table of a close relative you love. When you look at
the picture, you may not address it in words. But
you are uniting yourself to the loving spirit of the
person whose image you treasure. This too can be
considered prayer.

Let's call it by a very time-honored name: the
prayer of simple regard.

ANGELS ATTEND A BAPTISM

Recently my husband and I were sponsors at the baptism of an eight-year-old girl, the daughter of our friends Harold and Karen Fickett in Nacogdoches, Texas. As we gathered around the splendid modern baptismal font in Sacred Heart Church, my husband and I realized that the priest who was performing the baptism was elaborating the service with comments about the angels and the saints. "Your guardian angel is with you," he said. "I've been told that our guardian angels are the same height as we are. So your guardian angel is just your size."

It dawned on me that the priest was doing some instruction in Catholic spirituality because the little girl, Eve, was at a very teachable age, and clearly delighted with all the extra information he provided. We, too, appreciated many of the things about the service that were distinctively Catholic: the use of candles, the anointing with oil, the renewal of our own baptismal promises. Though Eve was the one being baptized, the priest was careful to include her older brother Will, and sprinkled him with holy water at a given point.

After the sacrament had been administered, we all went toward the foot of the altar, where Eve was encouraged to kneel and pray. Did she pray to her guardian angel? I'm not sure. But we were all touched by the ancient beauty of the sacrament and by the reference to hierarchies of angels and the communion of saints.

SAMPLE TEXTS

The Divine Praises

Blessed be God
Blessed be his holy name.
Blessed be Jesus Christ, true God and true man.
Blessed be the name of Jesus.
Blessed be his most sacred heart.
Blessed be his most precious blood.
Blessed be Jesus in the most holy sacrament of the altar.
Blessed be the Holy Spirit, the Paraclete.
Blessed be the great Mother of God, Mary most holy.
Blessed be her holy and Immaculate Conception.
Blessed be the name of Mary, virgin and mother.
Blessed be St. Joseph, her most chaste spouse.
Blessed be God in his angels and in his saints.

Christ as a light, illumine and guide me.
Christ as a shield, o'ershadow and cover me.
Christ be under me. Christ be over me.
Christ be before me, behind me, and about
me.Christ be this day within and without me.
Christ, lowly and meek; Christ, all-powerful, be
In the hearts of all to whom I speak,
On the lips of all who speak to me.

　　　　　　　　—From the Breastplate of St. Patrick

　　Lord, make me an instrument of your peace.
　　Where there is hatred, let me sow love.
　　Where there is injury, pardon;

Where there is doubt, faith;
Where there is darkness, light.
Where there is sadness, joy.
O Divine Master,
Grant that I may seek
Not so much to be consoled
as to console;
To be understood,
As to understand;
To be loved,
as to love.
For it is in giving
That we receive;
It is in pardoning
That we are pardoned;
It is in dying
That we are born to eternal life.

—Attributed to St. Francis of Assisi

Let nothing disturb you,
nothing alarm you.
While all things fade away
God is unchanging.
Be patient
and you will gain everything.
For with God in your heart
Nothing is lacking.
God meets your every need.

—St. Teresa of Avila

NOTES

1. *Positio: Informatio for the Canonization Process of the Servant of God, Cornelia Connelly (née Peacock), 1809–1879* (Rome: Sacred Congregation for the Causes of Saints, 1983), 107. Please note that this volume is generally referred to as the *Informatio.*

2. Kathleen Norris, *The Cloister Walk* (New York: Putnam, 1996), 30.

3. John Milton, *Paradise Lost*, book 1, lines 44–49, as they appear in Milton, Complete Poetical Works, ed. Harry Francis Fletcher (Boston: Houghton Mifflin, 1941).

4. Adler's work in philosophy was shaped by Thomas Aquinas. He is considered a neo-Thomist.

5. St. George and many other saints are honored by both Roman Catholics and Anglicans.

6. *Celtic Daily Prayer from the Northumbria Community* (San Francisco: HarperSanFrancisco, 2002).

7. *Celtic Daily Prayer*, 7.

Intercessory Prayer:
Petition and Intercession

Contemplation is an attractive and often consoling kind of prayer. For that reason we are often inclined to think of it as higher or more advanced. Yet the prayers of asking (petition) and of asking for the needs of others (intercession) are fundamental to the Christian life.

Notice how Jesus encouraged his disciples to ask God for what they needed. Jesus gives us this same invitation now. "Ask and it will be given to you; seek and you will find; knock and the door will be opened to you." And Jesus gives us a blanket assurance that our prayers will be answered. "For everyone who asks, receives; and the one who seeks, finds; and to the one who knocks, the door will be opened." He goes on to explain this promise in the light of the nature of God. Human fathers are generous to their children. God is a still more generous and loving father. "Which one of you would hand his son a stone when he asks for a loaf of bread, or a snake when he asks for a fish?" The argument is made from the lesser to the greater, from the human to the heavenly father. "If you then, who are wicked, know how to give good gifts to your children, how much more will your heavenly Father give good things to those who ask him?" (Mt. 7:7–11)

Jesus offers us plenty of advice about how to pray. His comments about the narrow gate are often interpreted as a teaching about prayer. In fact they are more nearly a counsel of discipline, of making a total gift of oneself to the way of God. "Enter through the narrow gate; for the gate is wide and the road broad that leads to destruction; and those who enter through it are many. How narrow the gate and constricted the road that leads to life. And those who find it are few." (Mt. 7:13–14)

HUMILITY IN PRAYER

Jesus' story of the humble tax collector is one of his most profound teachings about prayer. (Lk. 18:10–13) This goes hand in hand with his teaching about praying in secret, rather than making a public show of prayer. "When you pray, do not be like the hypocrites, who love to stand and pray in the synagogues and on street corners so that others may see them. Amen, I say to you, they have received their reward. But when you pray, go to your room, close the door and pray to your Father in secret. And your Father who hears in secret will repay you." (Mt. 6:5–6) Jesus seems to be saying that public prayer is not as good as private prayer. But his point goes deeper than that. His point is that God is really listening and that what matters in prayer is what God hears, not what others hear. Praying for show is prideful. Jesus is counseling humility.

He criticizes the pagans for the muchness and manyness of their prayers. "In praying, do not babble like the pagans, who think they will be heard because of their many words. Do not be like them. Your father knows what you need before you ask him." (Mt. 6:7–8)

Is this not an amazing remark? Jesus is teaching us to ask, he is insisting that we ask for what we need, and at the same time he tells us that the Father already knows what we need. Why, then, do we pray?

Of course Jesus wants us to pray. He insists that we pray. But he wants us to know that what counts is not a matter of informing God about our needs, like a spiritual grocery list. Instead it is all about coming before God in a sincere manner; establishing an authentic, simple relationship with our heavenly Father, who loves us and wants to bless us in every way. Our prayer is an expression not only of our need but of our yearning and our desire for God. We want a relationship with the Almighty. And Jesus tells us the relationship is possible. It is there for the asking.

LORD, TEACH US TO PRAY

When Jesus teaches the disciples to pray he is teaching us as well. The Lord's Prayer is not only a set of intentions for us to repeat by rote. It is a way of praying. Jesus is telling us what the disposition of our hearts should be when we come before God.

First of all we acknowledge the holiness of God. "Our Father in heaven, hallowed be your name." We affirm God's sovereignty when we say "your kingdom come, your will be done." These words express an attitude of submission before the authority and majesty of God. Next we admit our dependence, our need for God. "Give us today our daily bread." This expression of need and dependence is honest and straightforward. God is in charge and we are not in charge. We need God's provision and care. Next we ask for forgiveness, forgiveness that will come from God only when we too forgive the debts and transgressions of others. "Forgive us our debts as we forgive our debtors."

Jesus knows we also need God's protection against the evil one. That, too, is a fundamental admission that we are vulnerable. We are flawed and prone to sin. We need God to rescue us from our proclivities and inclinations. "And do not subject us to the final test, but deliver us from the evil one." Jesus goes on to underscore the point about forgiveness of sin. "If you forgive others their transgressions, your heavenly Father will forgive you. But if you do not forgive others, neither will your Father forgive your transgressions."

In all this teaching, Jesus has moved way beyond mere instruction in petitionary prayer. He is encouraging us to bring the right attitude to our prayer, one of humility, awe, and submission. We are not to pray in a flashy or an arrogant way, but with simplicity. He gives the same kind of advice about fasting and almsgiving, spiritual disciplines which are intimately connected to the life of prayer. At the same time he is teaching us about God's generous and forgiving nature. He wants to lead us into the presence of God.

PERSEVERANCE IN PRAYER

A further aspect of Jesus' teaching on prayer is his constant encouragement. He is like a coach egging the team on to victory. A good example of this is the story he tells about the persistent widow who constantly bothered the judge. "Then he told them a parable about the necessity for them to pray always without becoming weary." (Other translations say "without losing heart.") Jesus seems to suggest that it is the widow's persistence that gains her justice from the dishonest judge. Again he is arguing from the lesser to the greater, from flawed human nature to the perfect justice and generosity of God. "Will not God then secure the rights of his chosen ones who call out to him day and night? Will he be slow to answer them? I tell you, he will see to it that justice is done for them speedily." (Lk. 18:7) Jesus knows it is human nature to slack off in prayer. But he wants us to keep at it, to call out to God day and night.

THE POWER OF INTERCESSION

At church on Sundays there is usually a long list of intercessory prayers. We pray for our leaders; for the various concerns of our community; to be spared from tornadoes, earthquakes, and hurricanes; for our military; for world peace. We pray for the sick and shut-ins. We pray for the deceased.

But these may not be the only intercessory prayers in our Sunday Eucharist. We pray for our pope, for our bishop, and for our clergy. We ask for the intercession of the saints. We pray in company with the whole church on earth and in heaven. The Catholic tradition holds up to us a broad vision of the Church at prayer, including the Church in glory.

I like to think of intercession in terms of the seraphs mentioned in Isaiah's vision of God: "In the year that King Uzziah died, I saw the Lord seated on a high and lofty throne, with the train of his garment filling the temple. Seraphim were stationed above; each of them had six wings: with two they veiled their faces, with two they veiled their feet, and with two they hovered aloft.

"'Holy, holy, holy is the Lord of hosts!' They cried one to the other. 'All the earth is filled with his glory!'" (Is. 6:3)

A parallel occurs in the Book of Revelation, in which a vision of heaven is described. Living creatures are there with six wings, who are constantly caught up in adoration and prayer.

> Day and night they do not stop exclaiming:
> Holy, holy, holy is the Lord God Almighty,
> Who was, and who is, and who is to come.
> (Rev. 4:8)

This same moment is captured in the hymn, "Holy, Holy, Holy," in which the angels are "casting down their golden crowns upon the glassy sea."

Here, as elsewhere in the Bible, especially the Book of Revelation, there are depictions of the mystical church, founded on adoration and prayer. Adoration and prayer are realities—not visible, but invisible—when the Church is viewed as the Mystical Body of Christ.

So in Scripture and in mystical writing we have glimpses of how the prayer of intercession helps to create a full connection among God's people. This connection is what is meant by the term *communion*, which is used, not only for the Eucharist, but also to describe the nature of the Church: the Communion of Saints and Souls, on earth, in purgatory, and in heaven.

Can the modern imagination stretch this far? The practice of prayer strengthens our spiritual imagination and allows us to envision the Church not only as it is but as it will be. Prayer heightens our understanding; gives us glimpses of the transcendent; unites us in one mind and one purpose and makes us one in Jesus Christ.

William Law, in his book, *A Serious Call to the Devout and Holy Life*, speaks of intercessory prayer as a building up of the Church. This way of praying strengthens us as a body, links us to one another, and unifies us in Christ. As the old hymn has it, "we are not divided, all one body we, one in hope and justice, one in charity."[1]

Throughout the New Testament we find many encouragements to pray for one another, to hold up the needs of the Christian community before God. In the Letter to Philemon, St. Paul writes: "I give thanks to God always, remembering you in my prayers, as I hear of the love and faith you have in the Lord Jesus and for all the holy ones . . . " (Phlm. 1:4). Elsewhere in the Epistles, Paul advises us to pray often. "With all prayer and supplication, pray at every opportunity in the Spirit. To that end, be watchful with all perseverance and supplication for all the holy ones." (Eph. 6:18)

In another letter, to the Thessalonians, Paul recommends unceasing prayer. "Rejoice always. Pray without ceasing. In all circumstances give thanks, for this is the will of God for you in Christ Jesus." (1 Thes. 5:17–18)

We too can hope to become intercessors as faithful and powerful as Paul, who prayed most eloquently for those in his communities and under his care. These are his words to the Ephesians:

> For this reason I kneel before the Father, from whom every family in heaven and on earth is named, that he may grant you in accord with the riches of his glory to be strengthened with power through his Spirit in your inner self, and that Christ may dwell in your hearts through faith; that you, rooted and grounded in love, may have strength to comprehend with all the holy ones what is the breadth and length and height and depth, and to know the love of Christ that surpasses knowledge, so that you may be filled with all the fullness of God.
>
> Now to him who is able to accomplish far more than we can ask or imagine, by the power at work within us, to him be glory in the church and in Christ Jesus in all generations, forever and ever. Amen. (Eph. 3:14–20)

We do not have to be as articulate as Paul to experience the power and the grace of intercessory prayer.

SAMPLE TEXTS FOR PRAYER

There are many ways to pray in petition, intercession, meditation, or contemplation. These few Scripture texts are good starting points for prayer. There are many others.[2]

> You show me the path of life.
> In your presence there is fullness of joy;

in your right hand are pleasures
Forevermore.

(Ps. 16:11)

I call upon you, for you will answer me, O God;
Incline your ear to me, hear my words.
Wondrously show your steadfast love,
O savior of those who seek refuge
from their adversaries at your right hand.

(Ps. 17:6–7)

The Lord is my light and my salvation;
whom shall I fear?
The Lord is the stronghold of my life;
of whom shall I be afraid?

(Ps. 27:1)

In you, O Lord, I seek refuge;
do not let me ever be put to shame;
in your righteousness deliver me.
Incline your ear to me;
rescue me speedily.
Be a rock of refuge for me,
A strong fortress to save me.

(Ps. 31:1–2)

But I trust in you, O Lord;
I say, "You are my God."

(Ps. 31:14)

For in him we live and move and have our being.

(Acts 17:28)

We know that all things work together for good for those who love God, who are called according to his purpose.

(Rom. 8:28)

If God is for us, who is against us? He who did not withhold his own Son, but gave him up for all of us, will he not also give us everything else?

(Rom. 8:31–32)

Who will separate us from the love of Christ? Will hardship, or distress, or persecution, or famine, or nakedness, or peril, or sword?

(Rom. 8:36)

NOTES

1. From "Onward Christian Soldiers." Because of its warlike metaphor, this hymn has been dropped from many modern hymnals, but some of its imagery is quite tender.
2. See Thelma Hall, *Too Deep for Words* (New York: Paulist Press, 1988), which offers 500 short texts suitable for *lectio divina* and other styles of prayer.

8

Contemplative Styles of Prayer: The Simpler, the Better

WHAT IS CONTEMPLATION?

When I first began in the spiritual life I was influenced by reading Thomas Merton, a twentieth-century monk who taught that contemplative prayer can be practiced by anyone. Though Merton had "left the world" in order to pursue a life of quiet and solitude, he was strongly committed to the concerns of humanity. He was also attuned to God's presence in the natural world.

Merton's small book, *What Is Contemplation?*, attracted me to this kind of prayer. But I was never

123

fully instructed, at the beginning, in styles and methods of contemplation. I did not concern myself, for example, with measured breathing, praying in concert with the breath. I had yet to learn such terms as "lectio divina" or "recollection." I simply followed the advice I had been given: put yourself in the presence of God. I entered God's presence by an interior motion. You could say I just *fell into* contemplative prayer.

In those days my life was hectic. I was living in New York City, going back and forth to work on the subway, traveling to business meetings frequently by air, and at the same time trying to be a good wife and a good mother to three small children. I had a job to do and a household to run. The metropolis itself provided both excitement and stress. Anxiety was my middle name. It's no wonder I needed prayer. But I did not know I needed *contemplative* prayer.

I began by seeking times of silence and solitude. Sometimes I went to retreat houses to spend time with God. I took my Bible with me, using Scripture as the starting point for prayer. I loved spending time in Eucharistic adoration.

Without much instruction I began to practice what some spiritual masters call "the prayer of simple regard." I prayed by looking at or gazing on the Lord. I began my prayer time either by talking to the Lord, or by letting the words of my prayer drift away until I could come into silence.

When I couldn't go to a retreat house (because of my schedule) I would go into any open Catholic church where the Blessed Sacrament was reserved for prayer in the tabernacle.

Or else I would look for a "vest pocket" park (you can find them in Manhattan, small parks on city streets, maybe with a waterfall) or bench in an atrium or public place (a library, a coffeehouse) where I could come to quiet.

There were times when the simple experience of getting up early, before the household was stirring, gave me contemplative space.

Streaks of light were coming over the roofs and treetops. The birds were beginning to chirp. I felt myself in tune with the earth and sky, praising God for the wonder of created things.

Is it possible to become a contemplative in this way? I believe so.

GETTING USED TO SILENCE

I welcomed silence when I first stumbled into it. Silence was to me an astonishing gift of time, space, and peacefulness. Silence was for me (and is, for everyone) an opportunity to hear the still, small voice of God.

What I loved about Catholic retreat houses was that silence seemed to belong there. They are places of welcome and refuge.

I have since learned (mostly by leading retreats) that not everyone looks forward to silence. Is that because human beings are of different temperaments? Possibly. Or is it because we need to *learn* how to hold still, to *learn* quiet, to *learn* a peaceful spirit? I am not sure of the answer but I lean toward the second possibility.

Silence is strange to us. Do we rebel against silence? Silence makes us listen to our own hearts, beating. When we are plunged into silence we may turn our hearts to God.

Mostly, in modern life, silence is elusive. Silence offers the God-space we need, but it is hard to come by. The silence I am speaking of is a chance to hear the music of creation. St. John of the Cross spoke of contemplative experience as "silent music." The phrase in Spanish is *música callada*—music that is hushed and stilled. I am sure he chooses the phrase because it is a contradiction. The mystics are fond of poetic contradictions. What they want to describe is beyond description. But they give us hints and glimpses of a truth that lies beyond the humdrum and the everyday.

Father Henri Nouwen said: "The discipline of silence has been very important in my teaching. Last semester I offered a course in spiritual direction. One requirement was that students spend an hour of silence with a selected scripture passage. After that hour of silence, I invited them to come together in small groups and share what they had experienced. Many realized for the first time that there is something other than discussion. They would say, 'I was impressed that the Lord had something to say to me, and I was frightened when it happened.'"[1]

Listening to God may come naturally to children, but for adults it is a skill that must be recovered, nurtured, cultivated. We must accept and enjoy silence. Silence opens us up to a more intimate experience of God's friendship. To draw closer to God, we must practice silence. We must love and treasure the rare hush in our noisy lives.

Silence is more than a tool or a method. It is a pathway, a means, a curtain parting, a window into the knowledge of God.

SWEETNESS AND CONSOLATION

Thomas Merton convinced me that God wants to shower his blessings on us, and the best way to experience these is by spending time in prayer. "The only way to find out anything about the joys of contemplation is by experience," Merton had written. "We must taste and see that the Lord is sweet."[2] His comments were completely a match for my experience. I simply gave myself to prayer and God flooded me with consolation. Merton's counsel was like the reassurance I gained from reading Andre Louf. The gift of contemplative life (Louf had said) is already ours through baptism, not only because of the sacrament but also because of our longing and desire. Yet, we ourselves must cooperate; we have to open up to receive God's gift.

This spirit of receiving is crucial to contemplative prayer. To explain it, Merton uses such established language as "infused contemplation." In contemplative prayer God is infusing us with his love and grace. It is not what we do but what God does in us.

I was reminded of what C. S. Lewis says about his experience of coming to faith. For him, it was like snow melting. The ice block of his heart was slowly and very gradually transformed, with a kind of drip, drip, drip. It was not a huge dramatic change of heart but a quiet greening, like green leaves pushing up through encrusted snow after a long winter.

Lewis also says that in order to receive God he did not have to do anything. Instead, he had to stop doing. The doing, the activity, the acting was a form of resistance. He had to yield, to let go or give way.

From observations like these we conclude that the spiritual life is partly about our inner attitudes, our receptiveness.

"Be still and know that I am God." (Ps. 46:10)

CAN I BE SOLITARY?

No doubt many of us, when attempting the spiritual life, imagine and daydream about a mountaintop experience, one in which silence and solitude are readily available. Even monks cannot take their solitude for granted. Solitary experience has to be found and cultivated in a variety of ways.

It is possible, even in a huge metropolis, to be solitary in the middle of everything. For years I practiced this kind of solitude and cherished it, without fully naming it. In the roar of Manhattan one can sometimes go for hours without speaking to a living soul.

Yet to be solitary is not really a matter of being alone outwardly. It is a matter of being alone inwardly—alone with the Lord. This is a gracious state that can be discovered. It can be found. But also we must consent to solitude.

One approach is to create a space for solitude at home. This may be a formal space, a certain desk or chair. Or a space for solitude may be improvised: if weather permits, take your Bible, or your coffee cup, into the backyard. Wake up earlier than others and watch the sun rise. Go out at night alone and look up at the stars.

Mind you, there are special places—hermitages— where solitude is made to order for us. Nada Hermitage at the Spiritual Life Institute in Crestone, Colorado, is one such place. Those who live there year round call themselves hermits. But they welcome visitors and want to make the experience of hermitage available to them as well.

I think Nada's hermits will confirm what I am suggesting. Solitude is not only an outward but an inward state. It offers deep spiritual blessings.

Once, while making a retreat at Nada Hermitage, I signed up for Eucharistic adoration at four a.m. To fulfill my promise, I left my small hermitage about twenty minutes of four, with a flashlight, and began to make my way along the path from my hermitage to the chapel. About halfway along I became fully aware of my solitude. I turned off the flashlight and looked up at the sky, huge and amazing, with its abundance of planets and constellations. I knew that I was in the presence of an Almighty Power.

ORATIO, THE LATIN NAME FOR PRAYER

It is worth noting that the Benedictines speak of four types of prayer: *lectio, meditatio, oratio, contemplatio*. These are, of course, the Latin words for reading, meditation, prayer, and contemplation, respectively.

Not long ago my husband and I attended a summer workshop at the University of Kentucky for people wanting to speak Latin. Participants were from many different walks of life, but all had a love of the Latin language. I fell into conversation—in Latin—with a graduate student from Chicago. When I wanted to tell him about my writing, I used the word *oratio* for prayer. He insisted that the correct Latin word for prayer is *prex*. Later, I realized that, though Latin has two words for prayer, Christians had favored the word *oratio*, which means speech. *Oratio* also means conversation, and it conveys the intimate nature of our dialogue with God.

THE PRAYER OF RECOLLECTION

One can learn a lot from the Carmelites about prayer. At least four of the major mystics of the Christian tradition are Carmelites: Teresa of Avila, John of the Cross, Brother Lawrence of the Resurrection, and Therese of Lisieux.

Teresa of Avila was the reformer who introduced the prayer of recollection to others in her community. What is recollection? It is a way of coming to quiet, probably something like what is today called "centering." The focus of recollection is to become fully attentive to the presence of God.

Why was recollection so controversial at one time? Perhaps because many devout and well-instructed Carmelites thought of prayer as recitation, repeating formal prayers in certain kinds of sequences. As we have already noticed, much of Catholic prayer is formulaic in this way.

But the formulas are not the prayer. Prayer flows into and through the formulas of prayer. Prayer is an interior giving of the self to God, an entrance into the presence of God, a lifting of the heart and mind. This interior movement of the spirit—a fully intentional movement—is part of what Teresa means by recollection.

"Let's recollect ourselves," is an expression Catholic teachers of prayer may use from time to time. What do they mean? Let's come to quiet. Let's be fully aware. Let's come into the presence of the Lord.

THE WAY OF THE HEART
(DESERT FATHERS AND MOTHERS)

In the earliest days of Catholic faith some devout persons went into the desert to pray. Even now the desert is a profound metaphor for the silence and the solitude we look for in our encounter with God. At the outset of his ministry Jesus went into the desert for a forty-day fast. Many who want to imitate Christ attempt a similar experience.

The Desert Fathers and Mothers go by a special name: the *hesychasts*. They are known for a very profound and inward type of contemplation called the Way of the Heart. The term *hesychast* is connected to the Greek word *hesychia*, which means "rest." This desert prayer, the way of the heart, uses silence, solitude, and inwardness as a way of coming closer to God. But the central motif of desert spirituality is rest and peacefulness.

In recent decades the prayer of the hesychasts has been practiced through a special prayer form known as "centering prayer." This fairly recent name is being applied to an ancient way of praying, one which is akin to the prayer described in the fourteenth-century mystical text, *The Cloud of Unknowing*. Centering prayer is a method of focused attention to the inner life, which brings us into stillness and prepares our hearts to receive God.

Recently, certain critics of centering prayer have said that it concentrates on the self, not on God. But

M. Basil Pennington, in his book, *Centering Prayer: Renewing an Ancient Christian Prayer Form*, writes as follows: "Centering prayer, coming out of the tradition, is a way today of freeing us, uniting us and giving us room to live and breathe the very life of Christ."[3]

LECTIO (LECTIO DIVINA)

Lectio divina is a Latin phrase that simply means sacred or divine reading. But in fact it is a very specialized kind of reading. If you have a number of spiritual books piled up at your bedside for fruitful reading (day or night) that is all to the good. They will no doubt deepen you and bring you closer to God.

But *lectio divina* is a bit different from the reading of spiritual books. Lectio divina is a form of meditation that dips deep into Scripture by a very attentive path.

You choose a text—the psalms are very suitable—and read the text slowly, devoutly. You invite the Lord's presence as you read. After a time you will find yourself drawn to a line, a phrase. Enter the presence of the Lord in and through this phrase, repeating it silently or whispering the phrase quietly. Slowly let care and anxiety flow away and be completely still in God's presence.

After a time, return, refreshed by the peace of the Lord.

MEDITATIO (MEDITATION)

I was encouraged to read, in *Living the Mysteries* by Scott Hahn and Mike Aquilina, "There is no certified Catholic way to meditate."[4] How refreshing! Though the word *meditate* is used in the Psalms, no one is entirely sure how the early Hebrews used to meditate.

Sometimes the words *contemplation* and *meditation* are virtually interchangeable. Some people who say they "do meditation" may actually be practicing contemplative prayer.

In Catholic tradition, meditation is often a more structured practice than contemplative prayer. You may choose to read a written meditation by some notable saint or spiritual writer. You may take a passage from the Gospels, read it, and reflect on it. Or else you may write your own reflection on some aspect of your relationship to God. This, too, is meditation.

Whatever you do, it is good to set aside a regular quiet time each day. Be in God's presence, thank him for his goodness, voice your love. If you have before you a written meditation, read it, savoring the meaning of each sentence or phrase. Let God speak to you through the text.

ENTERING INTO THE BIBLICAL STORY

A vivid form of scriptural prayer involves setting the scene in your mind and entering into the story. A great many Bible stories lend themselves to this type of meditation. (Yes, it's another form of meditation.)

One of the simplest Gospel stories that might be used in this way is that of Jesus visiting the home of Martha and Mary. It's a very familiar, very small, and self-contained incident, told in Luke 10:38–42. Jesus is speaking and Mary is attentively listening to what he has to say. Martha is in the kitchen, handling all the preparations. She begins to complain about the inequity; she wants Jesus to take her side. Surprisingly, he says that Mary has chosen the better part.

Stage the scene in your mind: the small town of Bethany, the little house, the three persons in the story. Become one of the characters—say, Martha. How does the situation look from Martha's point of view? Play out the scene, the dialogue, let the event unfold. As Martha, do you feel left out? Badly treated? What lesson can you learn from what Jesus is saying? Are you resisting the message he wants to teach?

Possibly you would like to play all three roles in turn, until you feel you have fully absorbed the story. How have you profited from this meditation?

PRAYING WITH THE PEOPLE OF THE BIBLE

Jesus is the principal teacher of Christian prayer. Yet he is clearly praying out of a long tradition. Many figures in the Bible can also become our examples and teachers of prayer. We have something to learn from each of them.

Abraham   helps us to know what it is like to have an intimate friendship with God. His prayer in behalf of the people of Sodom is striking. Abraham was trying to discern the breadth of God's forgiveness and mercy to both the sinners and the saved. Abraham's questioning seems to fit with being close to God. Sometimes Abraham's prayer was mystical, as when he fell into a trance and experienced a terrifying darkness. Abraham also shows us that trust is fundamental to prayer. His willingness to sacrifice his son Isaac to God is a deep act of obedience, not unlike the willingness of Jesus to go to the Cross.

Jacob.   We know little about the character of Jacob's prayer but we do know about the fruits of it. Jacob's vision, a ladder of angels ascending and descending, came to him in a dream, but was the outflow of his prayerfulness. On another occasion Jacob is said to have wrestled with an angel of God on the road. The struggle went on throughout the night, until Jacob at last overcame God's messenger. What should we learn about prayer from this incident? Prayer is often a struggle to know God's will and to accept it.

Moses.   A rather detailed account in Exodus tells us how Moses engaged with God in prayer. God sent him to do great things, to liberate the Hebrews from their Egyptian slavery. But Moses felt unworthy and tried to resist God's command. This incident plays out in vivid dialogue. We, too, may have hard challenges put in front of us. The prayer of Moses shows us that prayer is an unfolding, sometimes an interrogation. In our intimacy with God we may sense a back and forth, sometimes even a tension. Notice the dialogue between God and Moses takes place within an environment of confidence and trust. The prayer of Moses should encourage us to be up front and direct in our dealings with the Lord. Also notice the many miracles in the life of Moses. All these—especially the water gushing from the rock and the manna falling daily from heaven—are signs of the profound love of God for his people, and for each one of us.

Miriam.   The canticle of Moses and the Israelites (after the crossing of the Red Sea) is a long, rich song of deliverance, of awe and thanksgiving. I have no doubt that Miriam sang it too. Miriam is shown leading the refrain of this canticle.

> Sing to the Lord, for he is gloriously triumphant;
> Horse and rider he has cast into the sea.
> (Exod. 15:21)

Miriam, a prophet, prays by striking the tambourine and leading others in a joyful dance. Her prayer is one of celebration, praise, and gratitude. These are good notes to strike in your own prayer.

Hannah   is thought to be the first contemplative. Because of her barrenness, because her husband's other wife was fruitful, she desperately wanted a child. But her way of praying was distinctive. She went into the Temple and prayed, quietly whispering for long periods of time. She was criticized because people thought she had been drinking. Hannah's deep prayerfulness can be an example to us. Also we should note her gratitude. She gave her son to the Lord, to become a Temple priest.

Samuel.   As a boy, Samuel takes a while to learn that God is actually speaking to him. But once he grasps this—under the instruction of Eli, the Temple priest—he also learns the right response: "Speak, Lord, your servant is listening." Samuel is a fine example of the spirit of attentiveness and obedience in prayer.

David   is the one to whom the Psalms are attributed. For prayer, we can readily adopt that view (no matter what the scholars say about who was the author of what). We know that David was a singer and a musician. We know that Samuel singled him out from all his brothers as the one who would follow King Saul as a ruler of Israel. The Psalms of David are an amazingly rich collection of prayers. David teaches us about rejoicing, wonder, gratitude, and awe. He also prays out of the depths and from him we learn that there are many moods of prayer. Sprinkled throughout the Psalms are many evidences of our intimate relationship with the Lord. "Behind me and before, you hem me in and rest your hand upon me." (Ps. 139:5) To pray the Psalms is to be nurtured by the same prayers Jesus knew by heart. This is a remarkable way to pray, one which has formed religious communities throughout the centuries.

Elijah.   I have often thought that the scene in which Elijah is fed by the ravens captures the way God feeds us in the Eucharist and in prayer. It is a brief story in 1 Kings. Elijah, who is a prophet, has foreseen a major drought. The Lord commands him to take refuge in the Wadi Cherith, east of the Jordan. "You shall drink of the stream, and I have commanded ravens to feed you there." (1 Kings 17:4) So Elijah did what the Lord commanded, hiding out east of the River Jordan. "Ravens brought him bread and meat in the morning, and bread and meat in the evening. And he drank from the stream." (1 Kings 17:6)

Isaiah.   There are thought to be three voices in Isaiah, that is to say, three different writers. Despite this change of voice, the whole book is a rich resource for prayer. God expresses his love to his people in a rich and vivid way. A text like Isaiah 43 is a fine text for prayer. It helps us to hear the Lord speak his love for us:

Fear not, for I have redeemed you;
I have called you by your name; you are mine.
When you pass through the water, I will be with you,
in the rivers you shall not drown.
When you walk through fire, you shall not be burned;
the flames shall not consume you.
For I am the Lord, your God,
the Holy One of Israel, your savior.
I give Egypt as your ransom,
Ethiopia and Seba in return for you.
Because you are precious in my eyes
and glorious, and because I love you.
(Is. 43:1b–4)

Hosea.   The book of Hosea is not long and all
of it is a good resource for prayer. Most people gravi-
tate to chapter 11, which begins with the lovely words,
"When Israel was a child I loved him." Again, this
Scripture is allowing us to hear God's voice as Hosea
heard it. The sweetness and the sorrow of Hosea's
prayer stem from the infidelity of his wife, Gomer.
Hosea compares Gomer's sin to Israel's betrayal of the
Lord. Out of this anguish come words that, all these
centuries later, move us to repentance. Pray like Hosea
and you too will hear the Lord's voice, forgiving your
sins and those of humanity.

Mary of Bethany   teaches us about attentiveness
and adoration. In the story of Jesus' visit to her home
she is attentively listening to him. We, too, try to listen to Jesus in our prayer. In John 12 the story is told
of Jesus and other disciples attending a dinner held in
Bethany. Mary takes a liter of costly perfumed oil and
uses it to anoint the feet of Jesus. Jesus defends her
action against the criticism offered by Judas. We would
do well to follow Mary's attitude in prayer. As I say in
the following poem, her spirituality is one of extravagant love:

Bethany

She knelt before him,
anointing his feet with
perfume
and wiping them with her hair.

"Tch, tch,"
said others,
"extravagant creature,
don't you know the value of a coin, these days?"
But he rebuked them.

Oh, to be that Mary
and to surrender
entirely to Our Lord.
To kneel before him
body and spirit
letting go . . .
. . . and the grace of his presence rushing in.

Mary Magdalene   can be seen as teaching us the prayer of sorrow and repentance. Scripture tells us that she is the woman out of whom Jesus drove seven devils. In the tradition she was thought to be a reformed prostitute, but no substantial evidence exists for this. Even so, Mary Magdalene is always seen as deeply loving, repentant, and grateful for the healing Jesus has given her. Her genuine love and tenderness are a fine model for Christian prayer.

Stephen.   Tradition has it that many of the apostles were martyred. Stephen, the first martyr, was stoned to death. His ordeal is recorded in the Acts of the Apostles, and the words of his dying prayer are also given there. "As they were stoning Stephen, he called out, 'Lord Jesus, receive my spirit.' Then he fell to his knees and cried out in a loud voice, 'Lord, do not hold this sin against them,' and when he had said this, he fell asleep. (Acts 7:59–60)

Paul the Apostle   was deeply prayerful, often thought to be a mystic. He constantly prays for others in the community and encourages them to pray for each other. He frequently uses the expression "in Christ" to suggest to us the way we are sustained in grace through our relationship to the Savior.

John the Beloved Disciple.   Through his affection for Jesus, John gives us a clue to the blessings of prayer. The Book of Revelation is thought to be an account of a vision given to the beloved disciple at Patmos, one of the Greek islands, where he lived out his days. Perhaps we shouldn't quite aspire to pray like John, for his was a rare gift. But such accounts of the content of prayer in Scripture should encourage us. We may not have visions as John did. But for each of us prayer is an entrance into a rich universe.

These are just a few of the encouraging models of prayer to be found in Scripture. As you leaf prayerfully through the Bible, you will find many more.

CONTEMPLATIVES IN ACTION

The idea that the contemplative life and the active life can coexist is often attributed to St. Ignatius Loyola. In establishing the Jesuits (the Society of Jesus), he argued that men of prayer could more effectively penetrate the culture and bring Christ to others without a restrictive and cloistered lifestyle. In a sense, he is one of the first who took contemplation out of the monastery and brought it into the world.

But two other important figures should be mentioned: Brother Lawrence of the Resurrection, a seventeenth-century Carmelite, and Therese of Lisieux, a cloistered Carmelite of the late nineteenth century. Brother Lawrence taught the possibility of practicing the presence of God in the middle of ordinary daily life. Therese made a similar discovery, which she called "The Little Way." This idea of being a contemplative in the middle of things crops up over and over in Christian history. It needs to be invented over and over again because it satisfies a definite need.

Contemplation is not a matter of being in a certain place. It is a matter of moving into the presence of God whenever you can, wherever you are. Contemplation is a matter of attention and of reverence, not of location.

To practice contemplation requires discipline and commitment. But contemplatives do not regard their prayer time as a burden. They are often swept up into the presence of God. They experience God's love and encouragement. They are refreshed by prayer.

EFFECTS OF CONTEMPLATIVE PRAYER

Admittedly, one ought not to practice contemplation for its benefits or results. Yet it is human to wonder, what's the good of contemplation? How will it change me?

Perhaps the principal good to be desired from contemplation is an inner peacefulness, a serenity that permits us to cope with the daily struggle.

My own sense is that a sustained experience of contemplative prayer focuses our eyes on the Lord, and lifts our horizons. There is a line in one of the liturgical prayers—possibly in one of the prefaces—that well expresses this. "Teach us to live in this passing world with eyes fixed on the world to come."

Contemplatives live in grace. While grace is the condition of all Christians, contemplatives are fully aware of their salvation and redemption and the beauty of the resurrected life.

SAMPLE TEXTS

The following psalms are suitable for *lectio divina*, leading into contemplative prayer. The method is simple. Read the psalm through quietly and attentively. Allow a phrase to draw you into the presence. Repeat or murmur that single phrase, prayerfully, then enter into the silence. After a time of contemplation, return to the psalm, and close with the sign of the cross and an Amen.

Psalm 23

The Lord is my shepherd; I shall not want
in verdant pastures he gives me repose;
Beside restful waters he leads me;
he refreshes my soul.
He guides me in right paths

for his name's sake.
Even though I walk in the dark valley
I fear no evil; for you are at my side.
With your rod and your staff
that give me courage.

You spread the table before me
in the sight of my foes;
You anoint my head with oil;
my cup overflows.
Only goodness and kindness follow me
all the days of my life;
And I shall dwell in the house of the Lord
for years to come.

Psalm 90 (1–8, 14–16)

You who dwell in the shelter of the Most High,
who abide in the shadow of the Almighty,
Say to the Lord, "My refuge and my fortress,
my God, in whom I trust."
For he will rescue you from the snare of the fowler,
from the destroying pestilence.
With his pinions he will cover you,
and under his wings you shall take refuge;
his faithfulness is a buckler and a shield.
You shall not fear the terror of the night
nor the arrow that flies by day;
Not the pestilence that roams in darkness
nor the devastating plague at noon.
Though a thousand fall at your side,

ten thousand at your right side,
near you it shall not come.

Because he clings to me, I will deliver him;
I will set him on high because he
acknowledges my name.
He shall call upon me, and I will answer him;
I will be with him in distress;
I will deliver him and glorify him;
with length of days I will gratify him
and will show him my salvation.

NOTES

1. A joint interview with Henri Nouwen and Richard J. Foster, originally published in *Leadership Journal*, 1982. Father Nouwen died in 1996.
2. Thomas Merton, *What Is Contemplation?* (Springfield, Ill.: Templegate, 1978), 23.
3. M. Basil Pennington, OCSO, *Centering Prayer: Renewing an Ancient Christian Prayer-Form* (New York: Doubleday Image, 1982), 59. On p. 112 of the same volume Pennington relates centering prayer to the four aspects of prayer mentioned in the Benedictine tradition: *lectio, meditatio, oratio, contemplatio*. He declines to associate centering prayer with any particular degree or stage of progress in the Christian life.
4. Scott Hahn and Mike Aquilina, *Living the Mysteries: A Guide for Unfinished Christians* (Huntington, Ind.: Our Sunday Visitor, 2003).

9

Practical Strategies

REGULAR PRAYER TIMES

Why is it important to have regular prayer times? Partly, it's reassuring. Like the lives of children, in which meals, naps, bath, and bed are at predictable times, a regular prayer time reminds us of order in the universe, and comforts us. But regular prayer times bless us over and above the comfort level. Prayer is transforming; it helps us get better, makes us more virtuous and on the whole happier. If you envision prayer as a rain shower of special grace, you'll want to be drenched more often than not. And if you think of that rain shower as helping the plant to grow and flower, you'll be sure of having prayer time frequently, at regular intervals.

Use all your ingenuity to squeeze prayer into each day. There are many corners of time in which prayer will work for you, corners of time that are currently gathering dust. When I worked in a major advertising agency in New York City, I sometimes prayed in the elevator. Escalators are equally well suited for prayer. Those are times when, without prayer, you wouldn't be doing anything in particular. Short, brief prayers—or recitation of a psalm—work well in idle moments like these.

What about noisy situations? These, too, are suitable for prayer. C. S. Lewis liked to pray on railway journeys. Many have prayed on subways and buses. It's a matter of concentration and attention. You can make prayer work almost anywhere. In a difficult environment—say, a prison cell—prayer lifts you into another and more beautiful realm, into the presence of God.

FREQUENT ATTENDANCE AT MASS

Taking part in the Eucharist is a powerful way to pray. Catholics are encouraged to attend Mass frequently and receive the sacrament often. The effects are transforming. One of the most important aspects of the Eucharist is the forgiving power of the sacrament. As the liturgical year unfolds, key passages of Scripture remind us of the essentials of our faith. Feast days come and go, and we are kept in touch with the excellence of the saints. The whole focus of frequent Mass attendance is positive and hopeful. We sense that we are on a journey; Christ is the destination.

SMALL GROUP PARTICIPATION

One of the most enlivening aspects of our spiritual lives is conversation. Many of the saints grew in holiness because of their friendship with each other. Today, one of the best ways to pursue such conversation is in small groups, sometimes called spiritual formation groups.

Many churches offer these small discussion groups with experienced facilitators and time-tested discussion guides. If you don't find such a group near you, you might consider starting one. Keep the content level high. Try reading assigned chapters of the Gospels and the Acts of the Apostles. Consider the Epistles as material for group discussion. Don't think of it as Bible study so much as an opportunity for spiritual growth and reflection. Begin every meeting and close every meeting with prayer.

What is the main benefit of small group discussion? I think such groups provide us with insight. For several years my husband and I belonged to such a group in New Orleans. The focus was on Christ in the marketplace. I was amazed at the way the discussion began small, with little insights, and developed throughout the group as one or another person had a turn. At some point, without warning, we felt a major insight bloom. Everyone went away refreshed and looked forward to the next time.

SPIRITUAL READING

One of the real blessings of contemporary life is that good spiritual books are so widely available. Every church library and retreat house has a good collection, and though you may not have a good Catholic bookstore nearby, much good spiritual literature is now available over the Internet.

On a daily basis, you might wish to consult the United States Bishops website (www.usccb.org), which puts you in touch with the daily readings at Mass, and some texts for the Liturgy of the Hours. The Catholic Book Club website is another fine resource. Reading Catholic publications will often put you in touch with good spiritual reading.

MUSIC AS PRAYER

Music is often deeply intertwined with our spiritual lives. And music helps us to pray. Often, at odd times, the words of a hymn will come to mind, even when we are not focused on music. Hymns and even secular music can become part of the wellspring of our spiritual lives.

Do you have favorite hymns, hymns you enjoy at church, but which you can't fully call to mind? It might be good to invest in a hymnal and use it as a spiritual resource. Hymns can be refreshing and encouraging in our spiritual lives.

Then there is other music that doesn't really qualify as holy, but which has a similar effect. I am especially fond of gospel music; some recordings by Sam Cooke move me profoundly. One of these captures a gospel story, the woman who followed Jesus so that she could touch the hem of his garment and be healed.

Some secular music has a profound spiritual effect. George Harrison, one of the Beatles, did a recording called "My Sweet Lord," which wasn't officially a religious song but was strongly spiritual. In the soundtrack of the romantic film comedy, *You've Got Mail,* is Harry Nilsson's lovely lyric, "I Guess the Lord Must Be in New York City," which suggests, to the spiritual observer, that a kindly Providence is guiding two people together in spite of their worst impulses. If we are open to God's love in all our experience we will sometimes hear his voice through popular songs and in other surprising ways.

Some of the best Catholic music—chant—is not often performed in church. We long to hear it. But if we don't, good recordings will provide us with this rich resource in the spiritual life.

What about music that you just enjoy? Music that isn't holy at all, but which you find uplifting? Spiritual directors often tell us to experience God's blessing in the things we love: books, films, works of art, dance, theater. In a world shot through with grace, we should not set up confining walls between the secular and the sacred.

JOURNAL KEEPING

Writing is a vital resource in our spiritual lives. Henri Nouwen, a great spiritual teacher, spoke of writing as opening up spaces within us: spaces we did not know about until we began to write. Writing is actually an aspect of attentiveness. We may not know what we are thinking or feeling, what the Lord is saying to us, until we begin to set words on paper. Do find a fresh notebook and make good use of this spiritual tool.

Recently I discovered this prayer by Kate E. Ritger for the blessing of a new prayer journal:

> Dear Lord,
> please bless this new journal,
> and the time that I spend reflecting
> in its pages.
> Bless me during my prayerful journeying
> as I struggle and grow
> and continue on my journey toward you.
> Its pages are now empty;
> unblemished, white, unlived.
> Where will I be when the pages are full
> —full of love, pain,
> bursting with happy moments and
> tears

Where will I be?
Bless this journal
and the time between its covers.
Amen.[1]

BLESSINGS AND DAILY LIFE

In some groups and families the only time that prayer is actually voiced is when the food is blessed at meals. This is a good practice, but the giving of blessings in ordinary situations should be encouraged and expanded.

Our Judaeo-Christian tradition offers a long history of blessing ordinary things. There are ceremonies of blessing for new houses, for new schools, and places of work. In fishing communities the fishing boats are often blessed. In agricultural life there are many spiritual songs to accompany work. African American spirituals are probably our best example. Celtic spirituality remains close to the hearth, and the earth, offering prayer that is very concrete and concerned with ordinary life.

Contemporary people may feel that such prayers belong to another place and time. But what about asking a blessing for our hands on the computer keys? And on the computers themselves?

To offer such prayers is to acknowledge Emmanuel—God who is present in the midst of things.

COMMON QUESTIONS ABOUT PRAYER

Over and over, as I work with people on the spiritual life, I hear them voice the same questions and concerns. Reading over stories of prayerful people past and present, I am learning that most of our prayer-issues are commonplace. Let's examine a few of the usual complaints.

A lot of things distract me while I'm praying.

Most of us have the problem of distractions at one time or another. Sometimes the problem is fatigue. Sometimes it is anxiety over the many things we have to do. Distractions are so common that we should not worry or blame ourselves about them. When we realize that our prayer has wandered from its main focus on the Lord, we should simply make our way back. There is no sense feeling guilty or inadequate because of this. Simply refocus, and return to praying. Be careful, though, that you have not set yourself too long or demanding a prayer-time. Short times of prayer are often the best.

Lately I have lost interest in prayer.

Recognize that prayer is a discipline, one in which the commitment often needs to be made over and over again. I like the expression used by Eugene Peterson, who says the spiritual life is "a long obedience in the same direction." Prayer requires energy. As we continue in prayer, we grow in our capacity to sustain a life of prayer. Think of it as something like athletic training; St. Paul himself makes this comparison. Recognize that you must re-engage with prayer and continue, even when you have lost heart. Start over again.

I would suggest that you vary your approaches to prayer in order to stay fresh.

What can I do to regain the joy I had at the beginning?

Probably you can't regain the joy you had at the beginning. It is well known that beginners in prayer experience special joys. The old name for this was "first fervor." The expression is out of favor, but the reality—a big flood of happiness at the beginning—is still around. Recognize that the shift in your feelings about prayer may represent a way of maturing in prayer. Be happy about the change. Now you have moved into a more adult way of praying. This more adult prayer has its own consolations. Be attentive to them.

Be aware that "feelings" are not critical to the prayer experience. Sometimes they get in the way. We should not be praying for the immediate consolations, but in order to accept whatever the Lord has for us on a given day. Be thankful for what you receive in prayer, even when you can't exactly call it "joy."

I think I am experiencing "the dark night of the soul."

Many people who have a sustained experience of prayer come into a time of dryness or darkness. This is one of the many moods of prayer. It is usually a sign of advancing in prayer, of coming into a close relationship with the Lord. However, this experience should not be desired or coveted. John of the Cross encouraged us not to cling to any experience or to desire anything other than God. The danger in thinking "I am experiencing the dark night of the soul" is that you are becoming self-involved or self-conscious, romanticizing your prayer. Be careful to focus on God and not so much on how you feel about where you are in prayer.

What is detachment and how should I approach it?

Detachment can be viewed as another word for simplicity of heart. When we are detached we are like the lilies of the field that Jesus spoke about. We are easygoing, lighthearted, unworried. That is detachment. To detach from things is to put your whole trust in God, focus on God, delight in God. Detachment should lead us to happiness. You will find a good description of this kind of happiness in the beatitudes.

What happens in the higher reaches of prayer?

The writings of the mystics try to describe this higher realm but often words fail them. Some mystics use the language of erotic love to describe their encounter with God. One of the best scriptural texts to describe this intimacy is found in the Song of Songs. There is a contemporary hymn based on the Song of Songs, which children sing: "I am my beloved's and he is mine; his banner over me is love."

Is it a good idea to read the mystics or to read about them?

Two books that provide a good introduction to the mystical path are by the twentieth-century writer Evelyn Underhill: *Practical Mysticism* and *The Spiritual Life*. All her writing is very evocative. Some of it is a bit old-fashioned, but much of it is accessible and she can also be witty and light in her observations. Underhill's books provide a framework for reading the mystics.[2] I have also written a simple introduction to the mystical life, which is called *Wonderful and Dark Is This Road: Discovering the Mystic Path*. I took the title from a fine treatise on the spiritual life which is called *Abandonment to Divine Providence*, by the eighteenth-century Jesuit writer, Jean Pierre de Caussade.

I think reading the mystics can be encouraging (so long as we don't compare ourselves to them and feel inadequate). Among my favorite mystical books are *The Cloud of Unknowing*, *The Interior Castle* by Teresa of Avila, and almost anything by John of the Cross.[3] Recently a fine book has been written by Gerald May on both John and Teresa, which is called *The Dark Night of the Soul.*

Another helpful mystic is the poet George Herbert, a seventeenth-century Anglican priest and a remarkable man of prayer. Though some of his language is difficult, most of it has a powerful simplicity that calls us into the presence of God.

> Teach me, my God and King,
> In all things thee to see,
> And what I do in any thing,
> To do it as for thee.[4]

SPIRITUAL DIRECTION

The growing practice and acceptance of spiritual direction is one of the best things happening in the twenty-first century. It is akin to the breaking open of contemplation as a gift for everyone. In earlier times spiritual direction was mostly confined to religious communities. Now it is widely practiced by laypeople as well.

Spiritual direction is an aspect of sustained practice of the spiritual life. This ancient practice of sharing one's inner life with a gifted and attentive advisor helps us keep our prayer lives on the rails, moving in positive ways.

The deeper your prayer life, the more you need a director. Directors are especially important for those involved in private prayer, silence, and solitude.

Remember that prayer should not be isolating. We ought not to become disconnected from the larger life of the Church. Prayer, even when we practice it privately, should connect us with others, not only friends and family, but strangers and the world at large. Prayer should make us more loving and compassionate. Spiritual direction helps to ensure that this is so.

Some people have extraordinary gifts in prayer, ways that the Lord speaks to them that are striking and powerful. Some are "told" to go to certain places and do certain things.

We notice such events in the Scriptures. But we should be rather cautious, both in seeking such experiences, and interpreting them. Spiritual directors are a great help in this way.

How does one find a spiritual director? Practically speaking, one should consult friends and pastors, retreat houses and houses of study. Even more importantly, if you need a spiritual director, pray for one.

PRAYER AND THE VIRTUOUS LIFE

One of the yearnings we bring to prayer is to become better people. The spiritual life should provide us with the grace to overcome certain faults. If we can't entirely overcome them, we can markedly improve.

One of the best prayer methods for growing in virtue is called the prayer of examen. This prayer is also known as examination of conscience or examination of consciousness.

Consider making time for this sort of prayer daily. If that is not practical, try to do this twice a week. Your journal may be a helpful tool in recording the ways you fell short, the spots in your life where improvement is needed.

Reflect on these during Mass, at the general confession. Mention them to your spiritual director. Or receive the sacrament of reconciliation. Do not be discouraged if there is a weakness or flaw that needs work and prayer over time. The spiritual life is partly about growing in virtue. We do this by receiving the boundless grace and mercy of God, and making good use of the graces received.

An excellent psalm for reflecting on virtue is Psalm 138: "Oh Lord, you have examined me and you know me." The Lord knows our hearts already, and will be merciful to us, no matter how we have failed or fallen short of his grace.

CHARITY AND SOCIAL CONCERN

A well-known hymn has the refrain, "They'll know we are Christians by our love." And one of the most stinging critiques of the Christian faith is: "See how these Christians love one another!" The fact is that a genuine prayer life should manifest itself in loving deeds. Our deeds and acts of service do not make us righteous. As Jesus has told us, our love of God is primary. Our acts of service are evidences of our love.

A story is told about the relationship between the British spiritual writer, Evelyn Underhill, and her spiritual director, the noted Roman Catholic scholar Friedrich Von Hugel. Underhill, who had a deep prayer life, was often besieged with self-doubt and discouragement. Baron Von Hugel advised her to turn her energy outward, by visiting the poor twice a week.

Other great teachers have counseled us to keep our prayer and social concerns closely linked. Christians who are involved in long-term social movements, lobbying and demonstrating for justice in modern life, should be careful to remain rooted in prayer. Dorothy Day was a famous advocate for the poor, the cofounder of the Catholic Worker movement. She was also a person of deep prayer, who always insisted that prayer should be the foundation of all social action.

One of the perils of activism is self-righteousness. For those seeking justice in a fallen world it is often difficult to see when righteousness has passed over into self-righteousness. One way to guard against this problem is to remain rooted in the Gospel. Of course, we should ask what Jesus would do today, and try to do it. But also we should study what Jesus said and did in his own time. Often, his greatest quarrel was with those who thought they had done everything right.

The British writer, Auberon Waugh, in his novel *The Foxglove Saga*, made fun of a devout Catholic woman who recorded all her good deeds in a notebook. (Apparently she wasn't nearly as good as she thought she was!)

Lady Foxglove looked up from the book and smiled bravely. . . . There were black circles around her eyes. . . . She took out her little notebook in which she wrote her day's good works. On each page was printed a little list: Bury the Dead, Visit the Imprisoned, Clothe the Naked—goodness, she must remember about Martin's new uniform—Give Food to the Hungry—well, that's myself, she thought humorously. She put two little ticks, once each against Visit the Sick and Comfort the Afflicted. The book was her little secret from the world, and nobody must know about it until after her death, or she might become spiritually proud, which would spoil it all.[5]

In this humorous portrayal of the virtuous life, Auberon Waugh is following the example of his novelist-father, Evelyn Waugh, who wrote a popular novel, *Brideshead Revisited*, about a devout and observant English Catholic family. Evelyn Waugh, a passionate convert to Catholic faith, brilliantly unfolds the story of the Marchmain family of Brideshead. In part, his purpose is to show the difference between authentic faith and faith which becomes destructive and domineering. I think both Evelyn Waugh and his son Auberon make the same point Jesus drives home in many of his teachings. Self-righteousness may look like righteousness to some, but God knows the difference.

Distortions of faith are commonplace. But they should not discourage us. Cautions offered by these two writers are reminders to keep perspective and a sense of proportion in our relationship to God.

A genuine life of prayer shows itself in simplicity, generosity, and kindness. "The fruit of the spirit," St. Paul writes to the Galatians, "is love, joy, peace, patience, kindness, generosity, faithfulness, gentleness, and self-control." These are the fruit and flower of the spiritual life, a life that changes us for the better and stands us in good stead.

NOTES

1. Kate E. Ritger and Michael Kwatera, O.S.B., eds, "Blessing a New Prayer Journal," in *Prayer in All Things: A Saint Benedict's, Saint John's Prayer Book* (Collegeville, Minn.: Liturgical Press, 2003), 33.

2. I have done a brief anthology of Underhill's writings, with an introduction of my own. The texts are relatively short; I have tried to show the arc of her writing over a lifetime. The title is *Evelyn Underhill: Essential Writings* (Maryknoll, N.Y.: Orbis Books, 2003). This belongs to the *Modern Spiritual Masters* series which features many other contemporary writers on the spiritual life.

3. I am the series editor of *HarperCollins Spiritual Classics*, which offers a number of the mystics in short, inviting texts. Among those included so far are Teresa of Avila; John of the Cross; the Quakers, including George Fox and others; William Law; and Meister Eckhart. A

series of twenty titles, with introductions by contemporary writers, is planned.

4. George Herbert, "Teach me, my God and King," in *The Works of George Herbert*, ed. F. E. Hutchinson (Oxford: Clarendon Press, 1945), 184. Spelling and punctuation modernized.

5. Auberon Waugh, *The Foxglove Saga* (New York: Dell, 1960), 29–30.

10

Spiritual Life in the Catholic Tradition

THE INTERIOR LIFE

Where does the yearning come from? I hardly know. I began to feel it urgently at a certain time—let's say in my mid-thirties. But was that the real beginning? Hadn't I been praying always, from my childhood? Not always knowing how, but praying all the same? Prayer had always been part of me. Yet my prayers had been stabs into the unknown.

In my twenties I had become a Catholic. It was a passionate choice, an upheaval, and a homecoming. Definitely, one thing that had attracted me was Catholic prayer. How had I discovered Catholic prayer? I'm sure it was a certain passage in Thomas Merton's *The Seven Storey Mountain*, in which he described himself, lying prone on the cold floor of the church at Gethsemani Abbey in Kentucky, and giving himself wholly to God. I was moved by the intensity of such a prayer. I was moved, also, by the community he entered, the Cistercians. I was drawn to their silence and their love of the natural world, touched by the romance of that contemplative community way out in a country place in Kentucky, carrying on a thread of tradition that had begun in Europe centuries before. When Merton wrote about the sound of the great bell at Gethsemani, calling the monks to prayer, I heard the great bell in my heart. I, too, was called to prayer.

When I first read those words—devoured them— I was sitting in my office on the thirty-seventh floor of the Tishman Building, a medium-sized skyscraper in mid-town Manhattan. I was searching, not for Thomas Merton, but for Jesus Christ. And I found them both.

What did Thomas Merton teach me? He helped me to see that there is something called the interior life. It was prayer, and more than prayer. It was an intimate friendship with God.

After I became Catholic, I continued to read Merton: *Contemplative Prayer, The Ascent to Truth, Seeds of Contemplation, New Seeds of Contemplation, Contemplation in a World of Action*. Catholics everywhere, Catholics in the world, with humdrum lives, taking the Long Island Rail Road, the Path Train from New Jersey, the subway from Brooklyn, the train from Westchester into Grand Central, people with schedules and responsibilities—we were all nevertheless reading Thomas Merton and in some vicarious way tasting the pure, fresh water of contemplative prayer.

Something else drew me (and Merton's other readers) to this contemplative vision. Prayer, we came to see, was no isolated event, no solitary enterprise, but rather a way of being engaged with the whole world. Soon after entering the Cistercian life, Merton had come to see that hatred of the "world" was a misguided thing. He explained how, when leaving the "wicked world," he had projected onto the city of Louisville all the sins that flesh is heir to; and when he returned, just six weeks later, cleansed by the intense and loving prayer of his novice days, he saw "how good is the city of Louisville and all the people in it." Like Abraham, he could see virtue even among the people of Sodom and could pray to the Lord for their sakes.

Something else impressed me about Merton: his encounter with prayer in the other great religions, how a Hindu monk at Columbia University had introduced him to monastic prayer, and how that same monk wouldn't let him become a Buddhist or a Hindu but insisted that he investigate his own Christian mystical tradition. Besides, Thomas Merton was deeply acquainted with Zen—not so much as a religious tradition but as a form of monastic and spiritual practice. And I remember being particularly struck by one short book in which he described that encounter. It was called *Zen and the Birds of Appetite*. In this book Merton opens the reader up to the nothingness, the emptiness at the heart of contemplative prayer. The "birds of appetite" are the birds of prey that hover to find a body, while Zen leads us to become no-body in the best mystical sense.

Oddly, these birds of appetite (ugly scavengers that they were) reminded me of more positive, biblical birds, messengers of grace that God sends to the soul. These divine messengers were like birds surrounding Snow White at the wishing well when she voiced her yearning and her dream. They were kin to the ravens who came to feed Elijah when he went to hide in the Wadi. As I began to discover the interior life I discovered a realm in which I would be surrounded by grace.

For years—how many years, was it eight? Was it ten? For years I had flirted with prayer, entertained angels the way Abraham welcomed three strangers to his tent in the heat of the day. (Gn. 18:1–2). For years I had daydreamed that such a gift of prayer could belong to me, and yet I continually thought it was not for me, not my thing, beyond reach, not meant for people in ordinary places and secular ways of living.

Yes, I went to church, faithfully. And I truly worshipped there, which was certainly prayer. But I longed for more, something intimate, a relationship with God on my own.

I am sure that this long time of reading about prayer and yearning for prayer was in fact, a prayer of desire. Desiring God was my prayer. And feeling myself unworthy to touch the hem of the Master's garment, that was also prayer, but I did not know it.

And there was no one to whom I could really tell it.

Who would believe this? How improbable was my dream?

Now, after many years of practicing spiritual life in the Catholic tradition, I understand that worship—Sunday worship, worship on feast-days and in ordinary time—is prayer. But taking part in the Eucharistic service is deeply intentional. In this way we enter deeply into the life of grace, what Catholics often call "the interior life." Prayer is not a matter of saying prayers. It is a way of living in the presence of God, not once in a while, but as a matter of course. This is the spiritual life, the interior life. And that, I think, is what Paul the Apostle meant when he spoke of "unceasing prayer."

DO I HAVE TO BE CATHOLIC TO
PRAY IN THE CATHOLIC TRADITION?

I became a Roman Catholic forty years ago.[1] For many years now I have been grounded in the Catholic tradition, but writing for all Christians. My writing has focused on the Christ-centered, Spirit-driven, Father-loving prayer that unifies Christians from many churches. But now and then I have emphasized

prayer-traditions especially cherished by Catholics:
the repetitive prayer of the Rosary and the litany,
contemplative prayer, fasting, the prayer of examen,
the use of solitude and silence. These are among the
many kinds of prayer long treasured in the Catholic
tradition.

Naturally you will ask: But do I have to be a
Catholic to pray in the Catholic tradition?

Obviously, the answer is no. Today, Christians
from many different churches are drawing on the
Catholic tradition and being refreshed by it, without
necessarily becoming Catholics.

One good example is Kathleen Norris, whose
book, *A Cloister Walk*, spent many weeks on American
best-seller lists. In this book Norris, in her deeply
poetic and often humorous style, captures her life as a
Benedictine oblate at a monastery in Minnesota, a life
that she took on without formally becoming Roman
Catholic. Norris explains:

> *The Cloister Walk* is the result of my immersion into a
> liturgical world, and in it I have tried to replicate for the
> reader the rhythm of saints' days, solemnities, and feasts
> that I experienced when I first came to St. John's in the
> fall of 1991. The book leaves the monastery, as I did, for
> family reunions, for work, for life at home in a small town
> in western South Dakota, and for worship at two
> Presbyterian churches there, Hope and Spencer
> Memorial. It also returns to the monastery, where for me,
> everything comes together.[2]

Turning the pages of Kathleen Norris's vivid account, readers find the richness of the Catholic spiritual tradition: biblical depth and insight, the wisdom of the early desert Christians, the ministry of angels, the communion of saints and souls.

A second example is Richard J. Foster, a Quaker who has founded a strongly ecumenical movement called Renovaré. Renovaré concentrates on spiritual disciplines found in the Hebrew and Christian scriptures. In his influential book, *A Celebration of Discipline*, Foster discusses twelve classical disciplines: meditation, prayer, fasting, study, simplicity, solitude, submission, service, guidance, confession, worship, celebration. I have worked with Richard Foster for a number of years, and I serve on the board of his organization, Renovaré, which serves Christianity in its multifaceted expressions. The Christian disciplines taught by Renovaré belong to all Christians.

Especially since the Second Vatican Council, many Roman Catholics have embraced aspects of Protestant spirituality. I am thinking in particular of "telling your story," a confessional sort of spirituality that can't be pigeonholed in one church or another. Of course, the idea of "telling your story" goes way back in the Christian tradition. One of the best examples of "telling your story" is the fourth-century spiritual autobiography of Augustine of Hippo, known as *The Confessions*. Many scholars suggest that Augustine originated this form of spiritual autobiography. Yet among many twentieth-century Roman Catholics, a certain reserve had developed. Personal stories of one's relationship to God were kept private. Now, for the most part, that has changed. It is good that many twenty-first century Catholics have learned to tell their own stories as a way of sharing faith.

In the last forty-odd years, many Roman Catholics have become more charismatic in the style of their prayer, praying sometimes with palms upraised, with hands held high, holding hands while they pray the "Our Father," and singing with real joy. Liturgical movement and dance has come into some Catholic congregations. Some Catholics have resisted these customs. Others have embraced them.

Meanwhile, many Protestant writers and spiritual teachers have begun to teach contemplative prayer and spiritual direction, two spiritual disciplines which have long been considered Catholic. I am glad of this. Christians from many denominations are opening up the treasure box of Catholic tradition and finding rich resources, resources that date from New Testament times.

Needless to say, Roman Catholics who share faith with other Christians might secretly wish that these friends could have the grace to become Roman Catholics. But a certain sensitivity, a loving concern, means they do not press the point. They are happy to explain their faith to others, even to defend it.

Sometimes they might even put their wish into words: "What a great Catholic you would be!" But in the matter of converting their Christian friends, they wait upon the grace of God.

The full practice of Roman Catholic faith is expressed not only in prayer but also in service and in sacrament; and Roman Catholic sacraments are reserved for those who are in communion with Rome, and who accept the Roman pontiff as head of Christ's church.

On the question of which Protestant practices may be considered valid by Roman Catholics, I must defer to the bishops and the authoritative teaching of the Roman Catholic Church.

Even so, I hope all Roman Catholics will have a welcoming attitude toward separated sisters and brothers, praying for them, sharing faith with them, loving them in Christ Jesus. And may Roman Catholics give good example to all their fellow Christians by eagerly practicing the spiritual life, being open to the life of the Spirit, fully living the life of grace.

OPENNESS

When I reach for a single way of describing prayer, the simplest word that comes to mind is "openness." To pray, we must open our hearts. We must trust first of all that God exists, and wants to know us, wants to hear from us. We must be open to interpret our experience in the light of grace.

Jesus tells us to become like little children. That is what we must do to receive the blessings of righteousness. Children are openhearted, sensitive, vulnerable, simple in the best sense. "'Truly I tell you, whoever does not receive the kingdom of God as a little child will never enter it.'" (Lk. 18:17 NRSV)

I think prayer also requires open-mindedness. There is no use bringing skepticism and gloominess and doubt into the life of prayer, no sense demanding proofs of God's love and mercy, no sense engaging in philosophic debating matches about whether and how God could be listening to every one of us, individually, all at once. To pray is to move beyond debates about the divine nature into a trusting relationship.

To pray, we must be openhearted, openminded, openhanded, filled to the brim with a childlike spirit of trust.

A wonderful expression is sometimes used by Christian philosophers and theologians. They speak of a second naivete.

The first naivete, of our early years, is behind us. But God calls us to a new childhood of the spirit. We may be intellectual, learned, sophisticated; but when it comes to prayer we look for a wisdom given only to childlike hearts.

Prayer is a yielding, a surrender, a giving way, to the God who wants everything good for us, and wants to fill us up with his love.

SAMPLE TEXT

Anima Christi

Anima Christi, sanctifica me
Corpus Christi, salva me
Sanguis Christi, inebria me
Aqua lateris Christi, lava me.
Passio Christi, conforta me.
O bone Jesu, exaudi me.
Intra tua vulnera absconde me.
Ne permittas me separari a te.
Ab hoste maligno defende me.
In hora mortis meae voca me.
Et jube me venire ad te,
Ut cum sanctis tuis laudem te
In secula saeculorum. Amen.

Soul of Christ, sanctify me
Body of Christ, save me
Blood of Christ, intoxicate me
Water from Christ's side, wash me clean.
Passion of Christ, comfort me.
O good Jesus, hear me.
Within your wounds, hide me.
Never let me be taken away from you.
From my evil enemies defend me
At my hour of death, call me
And let me come to you
So I may praise you with your saints
Forever. Amen.[3]

NOTES

1. I was received into the Roman Catholic Church on August 12, 1963, at St. Francis Xavier Church on West Sixteenth Street in New York City.
2. Kathleen Norris, *The Cloister Walk* (New York: Putnam, 1996), 30.
3. English translation by Emilie Griffin.

Index

About the Author

Emilie Griffin is the author of a number of books on spiritual life, covering such topics as conversion, prayer, retreat, and the mystical life. Griffin is a Roman Catholic who often speaks and leads workshops in ecumenical settings. Her most recent book is *Wonderful and Dark Is This Road: Discovering the Mystic Path*. She is the series editor of the HarperCollins Spiritual Classics.

Other Books by Emilie Griffin

Turning: Reflections on the Experience of Conversion
Clinging: The Experience of Prayer
Pope John Paul II Visits the City of New Orleans
(with William Griffin)
Chasing the Kingdom: A Parable of Faith
Once Upon a Christmas
The Reflective Executive: A Spirituality of
Business and Enterprise
Homeward Voyage: Reflections on Life Changes
Wilderness Time: A Guide for Spiritual Retreat
Spiritual Classics: Readings for Individuals and Groups
(with Richard J. Foster)
These Sisters Are My Friends: A Brief History of the
Eucharistic Missionaries of St. Dominic
Doors into Prayer: An Invitation
Evelyn Underhill: Essential Writings
Epiphanies: Stories for the Christian Year
(with Eugene Peterson)
Wonderful and Dark Is This Road: Discovering the Mystic Path